Supporting Transgender and Non-Binary
People with Disabilities or Illnesses

by the same author

Transgender Employees in the Workplace
A Guide for Employers
Jennie Kermode
ISBN 978 1 78592 228 2
eISBN 978 1 78450 544 8

of related interest

Transgender Health
A Practitioner's Guide to Binary and Non-Binary Trans Patient Care
Ben Vincent
ISBN 978 1 78592 201 5
eISBN 978 1 78450 475 5

Transition Denied
Confronting the Crisis in Trans Healthcare
Jane Fae
Foreword by Amanda de Courcy
ISBN 978 1 78592 415 6
eISBN 978 1 78450 778 7

Supporting Young Transgender Men
A Guide for Professionals
Matthew Waites
ISBN 978 1 78592 294 7
eISBN 978 1 78450 601 8

Counseling Transgender and Non-Binary Youth
The Essential Guide
Irwin Krieger
ISBN 978 1 78592 743 0
eISBN 978 1 78450 482 3

Supporting Transgender and Non-Binary People with Disabilities or Illnesses

A Good Practice Guide for Health and Care Provision

Jennie Kermode

Jessica Kingsley *Publishers*
London and Philadelphia

First published in 2019
by Jessica Kingsley Publishers
73 Collier Street
London N1 9BE, UK
and
400 Market Street, Suite 400
Philadelphia, PA 19106, USA

www.jkp.com

Library of Congress Cataloging in Publication Data
A CIP catalog record for this book is available from the Library of Congress

British Library Cataloguing in Publication Data
A CIP catalogue record for this book is available from the British Library

ISBN 978 1 78592 541 2
eISBN 978 1 78450 935 4

Printed and bound in Great Britain

Contents

About this Book

Who this book is for

This book is designed to help medical and healthcare providers, care agencies and individuals involved in providing support and assistance to disabled or chronically ill people who are also transgender. It aims to do two things:

- improve understanding

- provide practical guidance.

Many different disabled trans people contributed to the development of this book. As well as outlining the issues from the perspective of service providers, it provides service users' perspectives, exploring the difference between what is intended and what happens in practice. It explores the challenges faced by people who cannot easily fit into a one-size-fits-all system. It examines possible solutions and reasonable adjustments that can be made to better accommodate disabled people seeing trans-related services, and explores the way that prejudice and discrimination can be tackled to give trans people better access to services aimed at disabled people.

Why this book is needed

Trans people are some of the most vulnerable people in society. When they have to cope with disability or chronic illness as well, life can be very hard, and often the people who should be there to help actually make it harder. Many trans people have had such negative experiences with medical or care staff that they dread using their services. This can mean that they try to manage without until they reach crisis point, or, if they have no alternative but to access these servies, doing so can have serious implications for their mental health.

It is evident that many health and care professionals feel under-informed on trans issues. Some are actively hostile towards those they should be caring for. Some fail to provide appropriate support because they have bought into damaging myths. Others try hard to inform themselves and do the right thing, but don't know where to start.

Most of us will go into hospital or come to rely on care at some point in our lives. This shouldn't be any more intimidating for trans people than it is for others, and it should never come at the cost of a person's basic self-expression. Furthermore, young people who grow up needing care should feel safe to come out as trans if that's who they are.

'We have found that the NHS is letting down trans people, with too much evidence of an approach that can be said to be discriminatory and in breach of the Equality Act,' said the House of Commons Women and Equalities Committee in a report in 2015.[1] This book is here to help those who want to change this.

A note on language

The subject matter of this book means that you may encounter quite a few unfamiliar terms. A glossary is included at the end to help with these.

Because this book deals with subjects whose gender may be non-binary, uncertain or in the process of changing, extensive use is made of *they* as a singular third-person pronoun. Although some people find this grammatically distasteful, it is well understood, enhances clarity in this situation and has a long literary history, dating back as far as 1382.[2]

1

Sex and Gender
Understanding Transgender People

What do people mean when they describe themselves as transgender? Today, most people have a basic idea based on what they've read in newspapers or seen on television. With more and more trans people feeling able to live openly, the chances are that you've already met such a person in the course of your work, or that you have a trans friend or family member. It's difficult to try to understand a whole group of people based on a small sample, however. If you're going to be confident that you can provide an appropriate service to any trans person you come into contact with, you'll need a broader perspective.

Gender: what's it all about?

If you were born before 1980, it's likely that you grew up with a clear idea of what your sex was but didn't encounter the notion that you also had a gender until well into your adult life. It doesn't help that the word *gender* is sometimes used as a polite synonym for *sex*, avoiding the association with sexual intercourse; and it doesn't help that when talking about people, *gender* is routinely used in two different ways. To clear up the confusion, let's start by teasing those two meanings apart.

In 1990, the feminist writer Judith Butler penned *Gender Trouble: Feminism and the Subversion of Identity*,[3] introducing the notion of gender as something we perform – that is, as a set of behaviours most of us adopt in order to send a signal to the world about who we are. These could include wearing skirts, wearing make-up or going on recreational shopping trips with friends, for women, and talking about cars or going to football matches, for men. Of course, not everybody restricts themselves in this way, and some behaviours are considered more essentially feminine or masculine than others. This can also change over time. For instance, women wearing trousers used to be seen as shocking, but now it's unremarkable.

The other thing that can be meant by *gender* is the internal sense that most of us have of being male, female or somewhere in between. The strength of this feeling varies from person to person. Some women feel, for instance, that they could live their lives comfortably in male bodies if everything else was the same; for others, it would be endlessly upsetting. The prevailing opinion among experts is that this internal sense of gender develops between the ages of about three and five,[4] and in most cases it remains consistent throughout the life course (there is some evidence of change occurring in response to traumatic brain injury,[5] but few case studies exist).

For transgender people, the second sense of *gender* is the important one. In essence, they have a deep-rooted sense of gender that is different from what we generally expect of somebody with the anatomical features they presented with at birth. This can cause a deep sense of incongruence with the physical body, known as *gender dysphoria*. Trans people who have acquired physical disabilities in later life sometimes say that they find there's a similarity between their experiences of gender dysphoria and their relationship to their disabled bodies – in both cases, the body feels different from what their instincts tell them is *supposed* to be there.

'Changing gender'

Because the two senses of the word *gender* get confused, people often assume that dressing and behaving in a different way – at least if it was more widely accepted – would resolve trans people's problems. In fact, although it can help some people a little, it rarely resolves dysphoria. Doctors and psychiatrists involved in early attempts to help trans women were notorious for denying them treatment if they felt that they didn't behave in a sufficiently feminine manner – when, in fact, lots of other women didn't behave that way either. Trans women may still prefer wearing jeans, enjoy 'masculine' sports and work in 'masculine' jobs – just as other women do. Trans men may wear pink and enjoy romantic comedies. These behaviours don't determine who they are inside, any more than they do for anybody else.

The popular notion of changing gender is one that many trans people consider misleading because, by and large, when they seek treatment, it's not their genders they want to change – instead, they want to bring their bodies into closer alignment with them. Trans men, for instance, usually feel that they have always been male, even when other people struggled to recognise that. Increasingly, the science of gender development supports this contention.

There have, of course, been many people who have argued that it should be easier to change people's psychology than to change their bodies, but despite many attempts, there is little evidence that this has ever been successfully achieved. Perhaps the most famous case is that of David Reimer, who was raised as a girl after his penis had to be amputated due to injury at the age of seven months. Although this was originally hailed as a success and he went on to be given female hormones as he got older, Reimer began to have strong feelings that he was male around the age of nine, and went on to live as male from the age of 15. He suffered severe emotional problems in adulthood and took his own life at the age of 38, having spoken out about the harm that he felt trying to force him into the wrong gender role had done to him.

What Reimer's experience teaches us is that we need to listen to individuals when they tell us about their experience of gender. A recent study has shown that the simple process of supporting trans children to change their names and present as they wish to produces significantly improved mental health outcomes when compared with withholding such support.[6]

When trans people talk about their genders, they are generally referring to their internal experiences and not to any outwardly assigned characteristics. They may use the term *birth-assigned gender* (or just *assigned gender*) to refer to the sex listed on their birth certificates.

Intersex people, whose sex is sometimes difficult to interpret as male or female at birth, sometimes have their genders reassigned by doctors during childhood. Being intersex is not the same as being trans, but some people fall into both groups. Some intersex people feel that they have to go through a transition process because the wrong assumption was made about their gender; they may also have to deal with similar kinds of prejudice to those experienced by trans people. Whatever the circumstances of a birth, gender can only ever be assigned to newborns on the basis of what's most likely, because it will be some time before a child is able to confirm or deny it.

Everybody has a gender

Gender is a big issue for most trans people because they have to make an effort to get people to recognise theirs. Everybody has a gender, however. If you are a man with a male gender or a woman with a female gender, you probably just haven't had to give it much thought. Most trans people would prefer to be in the same position. Transition – the process of bringing a person's body or its presentation more closely into line with their gender – makes this easier. It's important to understand that trans people are not, as a rule, trying to make a fuss about their gender or get special treatment, but are simply trying to get into a position where other people cease to see it as an issue.

Types of transition

For practical purposes, there are three main trans identities:

- Trans men – people who were assigned female at birth but have male genders.

- Trans women – people who were assigned male at birth but have female genders.

- Non-binary people – an umbrella term for people whose genders are not wholly or consistently male or female, or who don't have a sense of gender.

You may also come across the term *cisgender* (or *cis man*, *cis woman* or *cis people*), which refers to people whose internal sense of gender matches the gender they were assigned at birth.

In practice, all of these groups are fuzzy round the edges. A cis man may feel that he has feminine aspects to his character and a non-binary person may feel more masculine than feminine rather than being right in the middle. Some people find that their sense of gender fluctuates from one day to another. Everybody is different and it's important to respect individual identities. When it comes to the provision of medical or social care services, however, these categories make it easier to group people by need.

How common are disabled trans people?

It's difficult to put a precise figure on the number of trans people in the population. A 2009 study conducted by the Gender Identity Research & Education Society (GIRES) in partnership with the Home Office estimated those experiencing some degree of gender variance at between 300,000 and 500,000,[7] but in the intervening years the availability of information about being trans has increased exponentially and public acceptance has also increased. There has been a dramatic increase in the number of people requesting referrals to gender identity clinics and, notably, the number of people requesting help to transition from female to male is now equal to the number seeking to transition from male to female – in 2009 it represented just 20% of the total of binary transitioners. This suggests that the 2009 figure may be extremely conservative. The Equality and Human Rights Commission estimates that 1.3% of people in the UK are trans or gender-variant.[8]

According to the Department of Work and Pensions, there are 13.9 million disabled people in the UK.[9] This means that, even if we take the most conservative estimate of trans numbers, we would expect there to be around 6,255 disabled trans people in the UK. Levels of disability are higher within the trans population, however, which would suggest a figure of 11,100. Given the likelihood that the actual number of trans people is significantly higher, this should be treated as a minimum estimate.

EU research has found that approximately 36.9% of disabled people aged over 15 need some form of care or assistance.[10] This suggests that a probable minimum of 4,096 trans people are currently receiving – or should be receiving – care in the UK. Again, the actual figure may be much higher.

Access to services

This book looks in detail at some of the ways that being trans, and experiencing transphobic prejudice and discrimination, can make it difficult to access health and care services. There are three key issues that factor into this:

- gender segregation

- prejudice

- lack of understanding.

Because a lot of health issues are, for the most part, easily divided along gender lines – for example, the vast majority of people who get pregnant are women and the vast majority of haemophiliacs are men – it is natural that some services will be divided along gender lines. Issues of propriety and patient confidence also mean that it's appropriate to segregate some services and treatment areas by gender. This isn't a problem in itself, but it's important to make sure that provision is made for those who fall through the gaps, and that non-binary people receive appropriate support.

Prejudice against transgender people doesn't always manifest in the form of obvious threats or nasty remarks. It can also have an impact on things like the priority given to looking after a trans person on a busy ward, or the degree to which a home carer is willing to help with personal grooming. These apparently small matters can make a big cumulative difference to an individual's well-being, or even to their chances of recovery from serious illness. Furthermore, some trans people are so used to being on the receiving end of prejudice that they anticipate it even when it's not there, making them hesitant to access services. This makes it important to be proactive in providing reassurance.

Sometimes, with the best will in the world, a lack of understanding of trans people's needs means that they are not invited to attend the right clinics or apply for the right kinds of support. It can even interfere with diagnosis. This is why it's important for individual health and care professionals to be trained in helping trans people, and why it's important for them to know when and where to seek further advice.

Respecting trans people

In most ways, showing respect for a trans person is just like showing respect for anybody else, but because we live in a society where trans people are not very well understood or very accurately represented by the media, it's easy to make mistakes. Most trans people understand this and try to take it in their stride, but when you are dealing with people who may be additionally vulnerable because of their disability or state of health, the last thing you want to do is risk adding to their stress levels.

On the most basic level, it's important that you respect trans people's genders in the titles and pronouns that you use to refer to them and the way you describe them to others. Where relevant, you should simply describe them as men or women (unless they are non-binary) and not use 'trans' as a prefix unless it's specifically relevant to the situation (as is the case in most of this book). Never reveal that they are trans to other people without their express permission, unless you need to do so in an emergency (e.g. if somebody you provide care for is rushed to hospital unconscious and you need to make sure that appropriate treatment is administered). When you talk about the past, don't use a different gender unless they have told you that that's what they prefer – for example, if you need to know the history of a trans woman's persistent eczema, ask her if it started when she was a girl, not when she was a boy.

Remember that trans people are people first, not learning experiences. You may be brimming over with questions but you shouldn't ask them anything that you wouldn't consider it appropriate to ask a cis person. Unless you are providing intimate care or treating a genito-urinary complaint, it is never appropriate to ask about genitals. Unless it's directly relevant to the service you're providing, don't ask about their experience of hormones or surgery. There are usually better ways to make small talk.

Don't gossip about trans people. You may be surprised how many trans people have overheard staff whispering about them in hospitals and other healthcare facilities. Even if it's not overtly hostile, it can make them feel very unsafe.

Never assume that someone is trans unless that information has been disclosed to you. Some cis women just happen to have big shoulders or prefer traditionally masculine clothes. Some cis men enjoy having long hair, or suffer from gynaecomastia (spontaneous breast growth). Being misgendered is no fun for anyone, and cis people deserve respect too!

Mind your language

Using respectful language isn't just about getting pronouns right and using people's chosen names. There are also other issues to bear in mind.

Transgender and *trans* are umbrella terms accepted by most of the people they're used to refer to, but some people who have gone through binary transition prefer the term *transexual*, because it distinguishes them from people who they feel have very different experiences. Others expressly dislike *transexual* because they feel that its use leads to people falsely conflating transness with sexual orientation. The safest approach is simply to use *trans* unless advised otherwise. Remember that neither *trans* nor *transgender* is a noun – they don't define everything about people, but just reflect one aspect of who they are, so one might say *trans people* the same way one says *tall people* or *shy people*. Don't run the words together, as that creates the same problem – say (and write) *trans man* or *trans woman*, not *transman* or *transwoman*.

The terms *tranny* and *shemale* should be avoided. Many trans people find them extremely offensive because of their association with pornography, and because they're frequently used as terms of abuse. You may overhear trans people using them about themselves or in banter with their trans friends. This doesn't mean that it's okay for you to use them if you're not trans yourself, any more than it's okay for a white person to use the N-word just because black people may be reclaiming it.

Non-binary is an umbrella term. Although some people use it as the main term for their identities, and most people are happy with it as an option on forms, there are many other terms in use, including *genderqueer, genderfluid, androgyne, agender, non-gender, bigender, polygender, intergender* and *neutrois*. Each of these denotes a subtly different identity but most of the time people will be happy if you can simply avoid addressing or labelling them as male or female. You don't need to remember long lists of terms all the time – just ask how the person you're dealing with prefers to be described and remember that.

Included at the end of this book is a table detailing some of the pronouns that non-binary people use. From the perspective of many disabled people, however, all third-person pronouns are over-used – they would far rather hear 'Can you manage a few steps?' than 'Can they manage a few steps?' addressed to a carer.

What the law says

Service providers should be familiar with their legal obligations in relation to trans people.

The Equality Act 2010

When it comes to trans people, the most important piece of legislation that service providers need to be aware of is the Equality Act 2010. This governs the legal responsibilities that organisations have towards their clients or customers. Specifically, it makes it illegal, in most circumstances, to discriminate against people on the grounds of gender reassignment. Although this might sound quite specific, there is judicial precedent for it applying to non-binary people as well as to those who are undergoing or have undergone (or are believed to be undergoing or to have undergone) male-to-female or female-to-male transition.

What this means in practice is that, as far as it's possible to do so, you should treat trans men just like other men and trans women just like other women. Provision should be made for non-binary people as far as is realistically possible – if you're used to the concept of making reasonable adjustments for disabled people, you can treat this in much the same way. You should ensure that all trans people have access to the same quality of service as your other patients or clients and that they do not have to put up with prejudiced remarks or other forms of hostility.

There are two exceptions within the Equality Act that have significant implications for some forms of health and social care provision. The first permits hospitals, psychiatric care facilities and similar institutions to offer single-sex services.[11] The second permits exclusion of trans people from the provision of single-sex services as a proportionate means of achieving a legitimate aim.[12] What this does is to give service providers some flexibility in challenging situations – for example, if a cis woman suffering from anxiety-related issues felt unsafe sharing a hospital ward with a trans woman because she perceived her as male, staff might be obliged to accommodate the trans woman elsewhere, but they would still have to find suitable accommodation for the trans woman (and not, for instance, make her feel unsafe or dysphoric by putting her on a men's ward), and they would have to demonstrate that it was the least disruptive solution available. If it could be demonstrated that the first woman ceased to feel unsafe after learning more about trans people, for instance, the hospital's argument that it had to deny the second woman access to the usual female ward would be unlikely to stand up in a court.

Under the Equality Act, it's still possible to discriminate against a person on the basis of a protected characteristic (such as gender reassignment) if you share that characteristic yourself.

The Equality Act also gives rise to the Public Sector Equality Duty, which obliges public authorities, such as NHS trusts, to take a positive role in advancing equality. This means that they must eliminate discrimination, harassment and victimisation against people with protected characteristics; advance equality of opportunity between those people and other people; and foster good relations between those people and other people. This means, for instance, that it's inadequate to respond to an incident of transphobia on a hospital ward simply by moving the aggressor to another ward – the behaviour itself should be directly addressed and the aggressor encouraged to learn more about trans people and be more considerate towards them.

The Gender Recognition Act 2004

The Gender Recognition Act 2004 is a piece of legislation that was designed to make it easier for trans people to access their rights after transition. Using this legislation, a trans person whose identity is approved by a panel of experts will be awarded a gender recognition certificate (sometimes abbreviated to GRC). With this certificate, they can apply for an amended birth certificate (recognising that their gender was misidentified when they were born), marry or form a civil partnership in their new gender role, and apply to receive a pension in accordance with that.

Not every trans person has, or will obtain, a gender recognition certificate. In Northern Ireland, married trans people are first obliged to divorce, and civilly partnered trans people are required to dissolve their partnerships. Some people feel that this is against their principles or don't want to do it because of the distress it would cause to their loved ones. They may also hesitate because it can have a knock-on impact on pension entitlements.

Elsewhere in the UK, divorce is not a requirement, but a married trans person and their spouse have to fill out a statutory declaration form to confirm that they agree to stay together, and the spouse has the option of using the request for gender transition as grounds for divorce. If one or both spouses wish(es) to end the marriage, or if the statutory declaration is not filled out, the trans person will receive an interim gender recognition certificate. In Scotland, this can (with the permission of the Sheriff court) be immediately converted into a full certificate (effectively meaning that the declaration requirement is moot). In England and Wales, it can only be converted into a full certificate after a divorce has been finalised. There is concern that this dependency on spousal cooperation can place trans people with abusive partners at risk.

Civilly partnered people living in England, Scotland or Wales have the option of either dissolving their civil partnerships or converting them into marriages in order to be eligible for gender recognition certificates.

There is, at the time of writing, no gender recognition certificate system to acknowledge the gender of non-binary people in the UK. Intersex people are not allowed to use the gender recognition certificate process even if they have changed the gender role in which they live from the one assigned to them when they were children.

Where the assessment panel has decided that an individual should not receive a gender recognition certificate, there is no right of appeal.

Some trans people simply feel that it is not the business of the state to give them permission to be themselves, and do not use the gender recognition certificate process for this reason. Others worry that having a certificate can mark them out as trans in government records and could therefore make them vulnerable if a government hostile to trans people came into power. They cite the way that registration of ethnic status has been used to single people out for discrimination in some parts of the world. This can be a particular issue for people from countries with a recent record of such behaviour.

These issues mean that it's important not to insist on a gender recognition certificate as proof of gender or as proof that a transition process has been completed. The provisions of the Equality Act are not dependent on the existence of such a certificate.

Applying for a gender recognition certificate requires cooperation on the part of medical professionals. A two-year 'real-life experience' test is process is required – see Chapter 4 on the transition process for details of how problematic this can be for disabled people. Doctors supporting people with disabilities or chronic illnesses can help by submitting evidence explaining why they have difficulty with it. If the applicant is unable to take hormones or unable to have surgery for medical reasons, a doctor will be required to support the application by explaining this, as both are normally expected.

Sadly, some trans people report that their GPs refuse to cooperate with this process and that as a result it is very difficult for them to achieve legal gender recognition.

Hate crime laws

Hate crime laws apply to acts that are already criminal – such as assault or threatening behaviour – when those acts are exacerbated by prejudice relating to specific protected characteristics. They differ in different parts of the United Kingdom.

Hate crime laws are not intended to send the message that some people deserve more protection than others. Rather, they are intended to communicate that prejudice itself is wrong and can be an aggravating factor in a crime. Crimes motivated by prejudice don't just harm their immediate targets but also intimidate other people with the same characteristics. An attack on a trans person, for instance, can make other trans people living in the same area afraid to go out, if it's clear that the assailant had a transphobic motive. Such crimes don't always happen face to face – they might take the form of damage to property with graffiti that makes the motive clear, or they could involve threats made over the internet.

In England and Wales, a crime is a hate crime if the person committing it is motivated by prejudice against transgender identity. It doesn't matter who the target is; what matters is what the perpetrator believes. This means that non-binary people as well as trans men and trans women are protected by the law. It also means that a non-trans person who is mistakenly thought to be trans is protected by the law.

In addition to this, a crime is a hate crime if it takes place because of the target's association with a person who has a protected characteristic. This means that if you are threatened by somebody who doesn't like your support of a trans client, for instance, you could be the victim of a hate crime.

Because a lot of people don't understand the difference between gender and sexual orientation, trans people are often victims of homophobic hate crimes. It's important to be able to distinguish the type of prejudice involved if a case goes to court.

Hate crimes are usually identified as such for one of three reasons:

- The language used by the perpetrator when the crime is being committed – this makes it important to pay attention and make notes of this as soon as possible.

- Prejudice the perpetrator has displayed previously that can be connected to the incident – for instance, if they told friends that they were going to go and beat up a trans person.

- Prejudice raised by the perpetrator when talking about what they have done – whether they are boasting to friends or confessing to the police.

In Scotland, the definition of transgender identity used in hate crime law is very expansive, explicitly covering trans men, trans women and non-binary people. It also extends to cover intersex people. People who are mistaken for trans people and people who are targeted because of their association with trans people can be victims of hate crimes just as they can in England and Wales. It's possible to prosecute a crime as a hate crime on the basis of any two protected characteristics, so if it's not clear whether someone was targeted because they were recognised as trans or because they were assumed to be gay, lesbian or bisexual, a prosecution can still be successful.

In Northern Ireland, being transgender has only recently been included as a protected characteristic in hate crime law. It is limited to offences committed against people who are themselves trans, are cross-dressers, or are believed by the perpetrator to fall into one of these groups.

Anybody can report a hate crime. Because it may result in witnesses having to go to court, you should discuss it with the person who was targeted first, to see what they want to do. Bear in mind that for people with some disabilities there can be significant barriers to accessing the court system. If one of the people you provide care for has been targeted and thinks it should be reported but doesn't feel up to dealing with the police straight away, you can step in to make the initial report, even if you didn't witness the incident directly.

Disabled trans people and human rights

There are several key principles in human rights law that apply to disabled trans people. Under the United Nations Universal Declaration of Human Rights,[13] the following have particular relevance:

> **Article 1.** All human beings are born free and equal in dignity and rights. They are endowed with reason and conscience and should act towards one another in a spirit of brotherhood.

> **Article 12.** No one shall be subjected to arbitrary interference with his privacy, family, home or correspondence, nor to attacks upon his honour and reputation. Everyone has the right to the protection of the law against such interference or attacks.

> **Article 22.** Everyone, as a member of society, has the right to social security and is entitled to realization, through national effort and international co-operation and in accordance with the organization and resources of each State, of the economic,

social and cultural rights indispensable for his dignity and the free development of his personality.

Article 25(1). Everyone has the right to a standard of living adequate for the health and well-being of himself and of his family, including food, clothing, housing and medical care and necessary social services, and the right to security in the event of unemployment, sickness, disability, widowhood, old age or other lack of livelihood in circumstances beyond his control.

What these articles make clear is that trans and disabled people have a right to be protected from prejudice and discrimination simply because they are human; that they have a right to support (insofar as the state can afford to provide it) if they are unable to work; that they have a right to medical care; and that they have the right to be their authentic selves. No trans person is any less entitled to freely develop their personality, for instance, because they are disabled. No disabled person is any less entitled to security and medical care because they are trans.

The European Convention on Human Rights[14] refined these principles with the aim of creating a tool that individuals could use to challenge their governments (although in practice few people can afford to do this and the few cases taken are supported by human rights non-governmental organisations (NGOs), which usually prioritise them on the basis of trying to establish precedent that will help large numbers of people). Of particular significance are the following:

Article 8. Right to respect for private and family life.
1. Everyone has the right to respect for his private and family life, his home and his correspondence. 2. There shall be no interference by a public authority with the exercise of this right except such as is in accordance with the law and is necessary in a democratic society in the interests of national security, public safety or the economic well-being of the country, for the

prevention of disorder or crime, for the protection of health or morals, or for the protection of the rights and freedoms of others.

Article 10. Freedom of expression. 1. Everyone has the right to freedom of expression. This right shall include freedom to hold opinions and to receive and impart information and ideas without interference by public authority and regardless of frontiers. This Article shall not prevent States from requiring the licensing of broadcasting, television or cinema enterprises. 2. The exercise of these freedoms, since it carries with it duties and responsibilities, may be subject to such formalities, conditions, restrictions or penalties as are prescribed by law and are necessary in a democratic society, in the interests of national security, territorial integrity or public safety, for the prevention of disorder or crime, for the protection of health or morals, for the protection of the reputation or rights of others, for preventing the disclosure of information received in confidence, or for maintaining the authority and impartiality of the judiciary.

Article 14. Prohibition of discrimination. The enjoyment of the rights and freedoms set forth in this Convention shall be secured without discrimination on any ground such as sex, race, colour, language, religion, political or other opinion, national or social origin, association with a national minority, property, birth or other status.

The right to privacy, in both documents, is important because privacy can be a life or death matter for trans people and it's one that health and care practitioners need to take seriously. Although an increasing number of people are choosing to live openly as trans, others can face family rejection, harassment and violence if their trans status is exposed, and disabled people are especially vulnerable in this regard.

Article 10 of the European Convention is frequently cited in defence of freedom of speech (though anyone using this to justify prejudiced speech should pay attention to the second part of the article), but it also covers presentation. It gives people the right to express their gender as they see fit, and the state (which includes public service providers) may not, under ordinary circumstances, interfere with that right.

2

Social Challenges Trans People Face

As most people realise, being transgender isn't easy. It can involve a taxing medical journey and it is made more difficult by prejudice which is endemic in society, including within the health and care professions. Being aware of this prejudice is essential to understanding trans people's actions and behaviours and providing appropriate support. The threat of violence is a very real issue in trans people's lives and they are disproportionately likely to have suffered family breakdown, domestic abuse, discrimination in housing and employment, stalking and harassment. This is particularly traumatic for those people who also suffer similar experiences because of attitudes to their impairments.

As a result of transphobia, trans people tend to be very cautious about their physical safety. They face a high risk of violence even as children,[15] with knock-on effects on their mental and physical health. Fear of prejudice can affect their ability to get out and about in their own neighbourhoods, their ability to participate in social activities and their willingness to engage with health and care services.

Understanding anti-trans prejudice

If you've never felt any discomfort around trans people yourself, it can be hard to understand why other people do. Some prejudice occurs when well-intentioned people are misled by popular myths, but not all of it derives from simple misunderstanding. Some people are deeply uncomfortable with trans people on an emotional level, whereas others are ideologically opposed to their existence. If you provide care for trans people, you need to be aware of this so that you can help them to avoid potentially hostile situations.

Trans people occupy a difficult position in a society that already has a lot of hang-ups about gender. Trans men can make cis men uncomfortable in much the same way that butch lesbians do, because they're seen as encroaching on cis men's social space. This can lead to the assertion that if they want to live as men, then they have to be prepared to put up with casual violence and 'take it like a man' – something that is not pleasant for anyone and can present additional risks for disabled people.

Trans men are sometimes seen as trying to trick straight women into lesbian sex. Cis men are generally more hostile about this than women are, and more likely to struggle with the concept of how straight women can be attracted to trans men for their masculine traits and yet not care if they don't have penises.

Trans men are sometimes accused of transitioning only because they want access to male privilege and the easier life that it brings. Although many trans men report that some aspects of life (especially getting taken seriously at work) are better after transition, the fact that they also have to deal with transphobia means that life is often more difficult overall. The claim that they only want male privilege is particularly common if they have previously been members of the lesbian community, and (although most are supportive[16]) some lesbians view trans men as traitors.

Trans women can make cis men uncomfortable because they reject maleness and are prepared to give up the social advantages that go with it. Because those men might be attracted to them, they are also seen as a threat to male heterosexuality – men who refuse to accept intellectually that they are women, yet whose bodies respond to them in a way that's perfectly natural when a straight man encounters an attractive woman, perceive this as something that can make them gay. This insecurity is often projected on to trans women themselves through the assertion that they're deliberately trying to seduce straight men, or even that they've gone through the whole process of transition just so that they can do that (an old joke told by gay men about this attitude reflects that it's a lot less trouble just to buy such a man a few beers and assure him that no one will find out).

Hostility towards trans women is complicated by the fact that it's often intermingled with misogyny. Some people refer to the specific form of prejudice that emerges from this as *transmisogyny*. For instance, trans women are often told that they are not women but are, at the same time, subjected to crude sexual insults or threats clearly related to feminine aspects of their bodies.

More rarely, trans men can also be subjected to trans-related misogyny, especially early on in transition – for instance, being told that they only want to transition because they are too ugly to live as women (a variation on an attack commonly aimed at lesbians).

Even people who have come to terms with the existence of binary trans people and are happy to make space for them within society can be hostile towards non-binary people because they see them as individuals who are being awkward for the sake of it.

In addition to this, some people are ideologically opposed to the existence of trans people. There are two main groups that take this position. The first is composed of right-wing evangelical Christians. The second is composed of people – mostly women – who consider themselves to be radical feminists and see trans people as innately damaging to feminism or, more directly, to women. Members of this latter group are often referred to as TERFs (trans-exclusive radical feminists), but some consider this offensive. They have traditionally been associated with left-wing politics, but members of both groups have recently been working to coordinate campaigns against trans rights through the organisation Hands Across the Aisle.[17]

It's worth noting that the majority of feminists are accepting of trans people, while the majority of Christians, whether or not they feel that transition is in accordance with their religious principles, take a 'love thy neighbour' approach to trans people or simply don't concern themselves with trans issues unless someone close to them is directly affected by them.

Although most ideological hostility to trans people is focused on lobbying for or against legal changes (and, in some cases, healthcare provision[18]), this can include extensive messaging through traditional media and social media which has potentially damaging effects. First, it can increase stress in individual trans people who feel that they can't use social media without encountering people who hate them for reasons they cannot control. Second, it can increase hostility towards trans people in the general population, sometimes by promoting ideas that are demonstrably untrue (such as the claim, published frequently in 2018, that changing the Gender Recognition Act would allow trans women a sudden right to enter women-only spaces – something that trans women had been doing with the full support of the law since 2010 and that isn't governed by the Gender Recognition Act).

Myths about trans people

There are a great many myths about trans people in circulation among the public. Sometimes they're repeated in newspapers or on television programmes. It's easy to absorb them without thinking, but important to see through them if you're going to work with trans people and give them appropriate support.

Myth number 1: trans people are just suffering from a delusion about their gender

It's easy to get the impression that being nice to trans people is about humouring individuals with an unfortunate delusion. Science, however, suggests that this is not the case. There is increasing evidence that some aspects of trans people's brains function in ways that have more in common with people of their self-identified gender than with people of their assigned gender.[19] Furthermore, there is no evidence that gender dysphoria goes away in response to psychiatric treatment, as delusions do in the majority of individuals treated.

Specialists note that the term *delusion* is usually reserved, in psychology, for beliefs that are demonstrably untrue. The sense of gender, being internal, does not fall into this category. Trans people are under no illusions about the physical characteristics of their bodies. In addition to this, there is extensive evidence that trans people have existed across a large number of different cultures for thousands of years.[20] Delusions are usually specific to a particular culture and period.

Myth number 2: trans people are just in denial about their sexuality

This belief dates back to the late 19th century, when homosexuality was frequently equated with men being more feminine and women more masculine. It centres on the idea that trans women are men who are ashamed of being gay and so find it easier to live as women, or want to become women so that they will be more readily accepted by their objects of desire – and vice versa for trans men. There are two key problems with this notion. First, trans people's experiences of sexuality vary as much as anyone else's – some people actually *become* gay or lesbian by transitioning, having been perceived as heterosexual before. Some people are bisexual both before and after transition – and non-binary people frequently find that none of these terms really fit them. Second, trans people face demonstrably more prejudice[21] and discrimination than lesbian, gay or bisexual people do, which raises the question: why would anyone see coming out as trans as a solution to either problem?

Although many service providers will consider it obvious that this particular belief is nonsense, trans people report that it continues to be a problem for them. Some have been told outright, by medical professionals, that there are no gay trans people (post-transition), despite being in that position themselves. Others have had their bisexuality raised as supposed proof that they can't be trans, being told that they are confused homosexuals and also – sometimes at the same time – that if they were really trans, then they wouldn't feel a sexual attraction to people in the gender role they wish to transition to.

Myth number 3: being trans is a fetish

This is a belief that applies almost exclusively to trans women and feminine non-binary people. In 1989, American-Canadian sexologist Ray Blanchard connected the two in the public imagination through his theory of autogynephilia, which asserts that some men identify as trans because they are aroused by the thought of their own bodies resembling those of the women they're sexually attracted to. This theory has been subject to significant critique.[22]

It's demonstrably true that some men like to dress up in feminine clothes in the bedroom, but far more difficult to demonstrate that this can lead to a desire to live full time as a woman. There may be various explanations for a correlation – for instance, some trans women may first cross-dress in this context because it's seen as a bit of light-hearted fun and attracts less social stigma than coming out as trans – but there is limited evidence that trans women are more likely to have a history of such behaviour than cis men, and little beyond speculation supporting the treatment of any correlation that does exist as indicative of causation.

The assumption that trans women and feminine non-binary people are all or mostly fetishists is damaging because it plays into other prejudices, leading to them being seen as hypersexual (which places them at risk of sexual violence) or sexually predatory (which places them at risk of other kinds of violence).

Myth number 4: being trans is a fad

When members of minority groups start to become more visible, it is common for members of established groups to experience a distortion of perception. leading to the impression that there are a lot more of them than really is the case. This distortion is amplified when the media gets involved. In 2018 there was something of a moral panic over the escalation in the numbers of children attending gender identity clinics, notwithstanding that this still accounts for a very small percentage of the population of children in the country (around 0.02%) and that many of those children will not end up going through a medical transition (the clinics are there to help children explore their feelings, not to point them down a particular path).

Concern was further fuelled by the publication of a paper claiming that coming out as trans may be peer-influenced[23] – a paper that was subsequently withdrawn by the university with which it was associated[24] after that institution discovered that it had been based on second-hand reporting by the parents of gender-questioning children through an online survey heavily advertised in online communities frequented by anti-trans activists. The World Professional Association for Transgender Health (WPATH) describes the 'rapid onset gender dysphoria' claimed by the paper as 'not a medical entity recognised by any major professional association'.

The increase in the number of children questioning their gender is paralleled by an increase in adults doing so, and is likely to be a consequence of social attitudes towards trans people gradually softening, together with increased awareness of the support services that exist. More likely than an increase in the number of trans people who exist is an increase in the number of trans people who feel able to live openly.

The lack of any solid evidence for social contagion theories should be considered alongside an increase in the weight of evidence pointing to a biological cause, such as the fact that where one identical twin is trans the other has a 20% chance of being trans as well, but this concordance drops considerably in fraternal twins.[25]

Myth number 5: trans women are a threat to other women

In recent years there has been an extensive media focus on activists who argue that trans women are in fact men and, as such, represent a threat to (other) women. Although it's difficult to disprove the contention that trans women are dangerous directly, as it's always difficult to prove a negative, the fact is that there's very little evidence to support it. Criminals exist within all populations, but there's no evidence that they're disproportionately common in this group, and in fact most trans women would not be capable of threatening anybody with their penises, even when they possessed them, because taking oestrogen makes it very difficult to get an erection.

Throughout 2017 and 2018, journalists searched hard for cases in which trans women had directly endangered women in segregated spaces, yet only one case, in the US, came to light. A study undertaken in the US in 2018 again found only one case, plus a case of a man who had entered women's toilets with no prior attempt to change his gender presentation and announced that he was free to do so because of a recent change in local laws – he was subsequently revealed as a provocateur.[26]

In 2018, an activist group publicised the fact that a comparatively high proportion of trans women in prison are in sex-offender units, but analysis of their methodology shows that their research was skewed towards prisoners serving longer sentences, which would be expected to distort the results.[27] In fact, trans women face a significantly higher than average risk of being *victims* of sexual assault.[28] Most major women's organisations in the UK support trans inclusion.

Myth number 6: trans people are a threat to children

There are two aspects to this myth. The first is that trans women pose a sexual threat to children; as discussed above, there are criminals in all communities, but no evidence to date that trans women are in fact more likely to sexually harass or assault children than other women. The second is that trans people try to persuade children that *they* are trans as a means of justifying their own existence. This mirrors claims made in the past about gay people. Although it is, again, difficult to prove a negative, there is little evidence for this beyond the fact that most trans people support the idea that gender-questioning children should have access to expert counselling and should not be condemned – a natural reaction from people who, for the most part struggled to find support when dealing with their own gender difference in childhood.

As a rule, trans people are very much opposed to the idea of anyone transitioning when they are not trans, expressing sympathy for historic figures such as Alan Turing, who was forced to take oestrogen because it was believed at the time that it would 'cure' his homosexuality, and who appears to have experienced a sort of artificially induced gender dysphoria as a result.

Myth number 7: there are only two genders

This is an easy idea to sell in modern Western society, but it falls apart when examined in a wider cultural context, and in the context of biology. Lots of cultures in fact recognise multiple genders, with those existing alongside men and women, including the hijras of India, the fa'afafine of Samoa and the two-spirit people found in many Native American tribes, and still more did so before contact with dominant Western culture encouraged them to adopt a binary gender system.

The notion that only clearly male or female bodies exist is disproved by the existence of intersex people. Sometimes intersex is dismissed as 'mutation' by gender essentialists, but it is a natural phenomenon as common as red hair, and it occurs for numerous reasons, including simple genetic inheritance – just like the presence of a Y chromosome in men. Bodies, like most things in nature, are difficult to categorise neatly. Social gender, as a system with its roots in the observation of bodies, is likewise variable, and as the personal sense of gender is internal, none of us can know anybody else's gender better than they do themselves.

Myth number 8: if society were more relaxed about gender, nobody would feel the need to transition

Many trans people would be very happy if this were true! In fact, most trans people do find that it's less stressful to be in social environments that are not strongly gendered, but dysphoria is about more than how an individual fits into society. Transition is usually about the desire to feel more comfortable with the self. This is why people endure the social trauma often associated with transition and increase their risk of being targeted for transphobic abuse, rather than simply seeking out communities where sexism is rare and nobody cares what they wear. The myth that social change of this sort would help trans people specifically (as distinct from society more generally) is usually put about by well-meaning cis people who don't understand transness as much as they think they do.

Myth number 9: trans people want to do away with gender

Although some non-binary activists (along with some trans and cis feminists) argue that gender is referenced in lots of unnecessary contexts, the notion that trans people en masse want to do away with gendered names, clothing, toilets and so forth is purely a media invention, used to create sensation and drum up sales. Trans people have to fight hard for their genders to be respected and as a result they can be passionate about defending their social significance. It's important not to confuse a call for a non-gendered option (as, for instance, with passports) with a call for gender markers to be done away with altogether.

Myth number 10: supporting trans people is incompatible with religious values

Although there are many individuals who use religious arguments to condemn trans people or the process of transition, no major religion is consistent in making this case. There are many churches, mosques and synagogues happy to open their doors to trans people. Hinduism explicitly includes legends about trans people in close connection with the divine. Many Buddhist scholars consider gender to be of minimal importance because it's part of the material world, when their focus is on reaching towards the divine. Sikhism disapproves of any form of body modification but does not turn people away as a result, and does not condemn trans identities. Baha'i traditions are respectful of trans people, although they only grant them the full status associated with their self-identified genders after a medical transition that includes genital surgery. Shintoism has traditionally accepted trans people; and trans women, like cis women, may become Shinto priests. Most Wiccan traditions are also accepting.

Myth number 11: accepting trans people is a threat to civilisation

This one might sound rather wild to some readers, yet it is taken seriously by many people. James Delingpole has described the acceptance of trans identities by the UK government as 'one of those pivotal moments in the decline of Western civilisation'[29] – rhetoric that resembles early polemics against feminism and against the ending of slavery in the US. This is clearly about more than the simple business of showing more respect to a small percentage of the population in order that they might live more comfortable lives. There are three concerns at work. First, that changing ideas around gender might weaken established power structures. Second, that a shift in the comparative values attached to information observed directly and information dependent on accepting the reported experiences of others might usher in a larger shift in cultural values. And, third, that any one major shift in social organisation might prompt people to consider others. At the root of all this is old-fashioned fear of change, reinforced here by the mistaken believe that transness or the acceptance of transness is a new phenomenon. Civilisation has gone through many bigger changes in the past without falling to pieces, and many of us would be likely to have far less satisfying lives if it had not.

3

Transgender People, Disability and Illness

Research has found high levels of disability[30] among trans people compared with the general population.[31] Nobody knows for certain why this is, but there are a number of possibilities. Most notably, trans people suffer from mental health problems related to dysphoria and the experience of prejudice, and they may compensate in ways that lead to physical health problems – for instance, by overeating or consuming too much alcohol. They also face a significantly elevated risk of assault[32] and face discrimination in housing[33] which means they are less likely to live in adequate accommodation.

People with disabilities face barriers to having their needs met across all areas of healthcare, despite needing more healthcare, on average, than members of the wider population. This places them at greater risk of developing co-morbidities and secondary conditions, increases the chance that they will engage in high-risk behaviours and increases their risk of premature death.

As this book will make clear, trans disabled people face increased difficulty in accessing hormone treatment, accessing surgery and being able to live authentic lives in their local communities. These factors contribute to poorer mental health outcomes, place them at increased risk of suicide, self-harm and addiction, and may have additional negative effects on their physical health.

Medical and care professionals can make a difference to this. By understanding the complex problems that disabled trans people face, and by being willing to listen, they can enable them to exercise their human rights, significantly increase their quality of life and fulfil their potential.

Transgender broken arm syndrome

There's a phenomenon in healthcare known as *transgender broken arm syndrome*.[34] It emerges from the experiences of many trans people who have visited their GPs seeking treatment for straightforward issues such as broken bones only to be quizzed at length about the hormones they are taking and their experience of transition. Of course, hormones can affect bone density, and doctors may also be concerned that trans people face an elevated risk of self-harm, but the point of the example is that the immediate treatment needed for a broken arm doesn't depend on any of this and 99% of such injuries will have nothing to do with the individual being trans.

Conditions that trans people report having been responded to in this way include the common cold, asthma, strained ligaments in the knee, epilepsy, stiff joints, chest pain and even Crohn's disease. Some say that they have had doctors insist on examining their genitals before agreeing to treat them for problems like these. In evidence given to the House of Commons Women and Equalities Committee in 2015, Terry Reed of GIRES described a case in which a patient with possible cervical cancer was referred to a gender identity clinic for a fresh psychiatric assessment before being referred to an oncologist,[35] the sort of decision that could have life-threatening consequences.

Transgender broken arm syndrome crops up in many different situations when trans people are seeking medical help. For those who have to interact with many different healthcare professionals on an ongoing basis because of their other health problems, it can be exhausting. It can also distract medical staff from the real problems that individuals are facing. For instance, a trans woman may be experiencing dizzy spells not because of anxiety about transphobia or the effects of hormone medication but because she has low blood pressure – something that would be among the first possibilities to be considered if she were not trans.

Disabled trans people are often treated as if their disabilities must have something to do with being trans. When a trans woman limps, high heels quickly get the blame. If a trans man develops a heart condition, it's often ascribed to testosterone, even if he's never actually had hormone treatment. Ironically, disabled people often complain that people see their disabilities first and not who they are as human beings. When they're trans, the disability comes second – but being human, and a complex individual, comes third.

Trans people as objects of study

Another major problem that trans people experience when coming into contact with health and social care staff is being treated as objects of study. Some may be happy to help you or your students learn more about what it means to be trans or how certain health problems can affect trans people differently, but not everybody feels comfortable being treated as a learning opportunity, especially if they're asked – or simply *expected* – to do it on a frequent basis.

Trans people often feel nervous dealing with strangers, especially in contexts where they're already vulnerable, because of their experience of transphobia. This means that they may feel extra pressure to go along with requests, and struggle to assert themselves. With this in mind, it's important to be extra careful about getting consent if you do want to use the opportunity to expand your knowledge. In a situation like this you should make clear that there will be no negative consequences from declining to engage, and although it would be useful for you to learn more, you appreciate that it could be frustrating for a trans person to be asked to answer the same questions all the time. You should also stay well clear of questions about genitals or sex – as you would with any other patient or client – unless your questions are directly pertinent to the reason why the trans person has come to see you.

Intersectionality

If you've had any kind of equality or diversity training, the chances are that you've heard the term *intersectionality*. Although it might sound more complicated, it refers to what is really a very simple concept: people can be members of more than one group.

In the context of equality and diversity, what this means is that an individual may be part of two or more groups that face prejudice and discrimination. In the case of this book, we are focusing on people at the intersection of being transgender and being disabled, but some of those people are also members of other groups – for instance, they may be transgender, disabled and elderly, or transgender, disabled and Muslim. Situations like this are much more common than many people assume.

Traditionally, where efforts have been made to accommodate minority groups at all, they have treated each group as separate from the others, as if there is no overlap. It's easy to see why this is problematic. If, for instance, a support group for trans people is held on an upper floor in a building with no lift access, wheelchair users will not be able to attend. If support services for disabled people are divided into groups for men and women, non-binary people will be unable to attend them and people in the process of transition may feel uncomfortable there too.

On top of this, there are specific ways in which the different types of prejudice people experience as a result of being in different minorities interact. For instance, trans men are often belittled because, early on in transition, they are unlikely to be as muscular as other men. Physically disabled people are often belittled for being weak, and these two experiences can compound each other, making it difficult for a physically disabled trans man to feel confident about his body.

Socially, trans people tend to be seen as hypersexual, and disabled people – especially wheelchair users – are frequently seen as not having a sexuality. This means that some people find the concept of a disabled trans person confusing, and some trans people say they have been told to their faces that they can't be both. Similarly, disability can be seen as negating the existence of any gender for practical purposes, because people assume that disabled people can't have sex, are unlikely to form romantic relationships and can't meet standard expectations of maleness or femaleness in terms of the way they present themselves. This can make it even harder for trans disabled people to assert their identities.

People who have successfully gone through transition are sometimes told that they are malingering when the subject of their chronic illness or disability arises, because a lot of people don't understand that these things are different – that while, for most people, it's possible to resolve some of the problems that may be caused by being trans, it's not always possible to 'overcome' problems caused by disability or illness.

People who are known to be trans but have not gone through transition sometimes have their gender called into question because of an assumption that everyone can take hormones or have surgery, when there might be medical reasons why that's not possible for them. People who are dependent on disability benefits may worry that if they are able to transition, then disability assessors will assume they are capable of working, even when that's not the case.

To ensure that they can help people with intersectional identities, health and care service providers need to make sure that all their services for trans people are accessible to disabled people and that trans people can safely access their other services. They also need to consider that trans people with disabilities or health concerns may additionally belong to other minority groups.

Advice for older trans people is available from Age UK.[36]

Advice on supporting black and minority ethnic trans people is available from GIRES.[37]

Being trans is not trivial

When people are living with chronic illnesses or with disabilities that seriously limit the way they can go about their daily lives, it can be tempting to focus entirely on those things and think of matters like gender as trivial by comparison. In practice this can have seriously damaging consequences. It's something that the medical establishment has woken up to in other areas – realising, for instance, that when a woman has a mastectomy to target breast cancer, her welfare will be much enhanced if she gets support to adjust psychologically, so she doesn't become depressed due to feeling like less of a woman. For most people, trans or cis, gender is a very deep-rooted aspect of the self, and it cannot be lightly set aside.

What this means in practice is that trans people need to feel safe to express themselves around medical and care staff, and need to feel that their gender is properly taken into account in the provision of treatment and support. This should factor into everything from record keeping to consultation to hospital placement.

Being man or woman enough

Sometimes the simple fact of being chronically ill or disabled can increase the dysphoria experienced by trans people both before and after transition, or can make them hesitate to transition because they don't think they'll be able to 'pass' in their new gender roles. This can lead to poor mental health outcomes and generally lower their quality of life. It's important for health and social care workers to be alert to these issues so that they can provide support where possible and avoid saying or doing things that might make them worse.

This is similar in many ways to reassuring cis men and women with chronic illnesses or disabilities that they are not failing to be 'proper' men or women as a result. It should only be done in response to direct expressions of dissatisfaction from the individual concerned. Never introduce the topic yourself, as this can suggest that *you* think there's a problem where the disabled person might not have perceived one.

What makes a man?

Two of the factors that Western society most strongly associates with maleness are physical strength and assertiveness. This can create a lot of worry for trans men who feel the need to express their masculinity clearly but who are physically weak, have limited mobility or experience social anxiety. Trans men with disabilities may also struggle to project their voices in the manner generally expected of men, and may feel that their ability to perform their gender is compromised if they are unable to take an active role in sexual activity (although, as with cis men, this may or may not be their personal preference).

When somebody is struggling in this way and wants reassurance, it can be helpful to talk about other positive characteristics associated with masculinity that relate to what they *can* do. For instance, a man with reduced muscle mass might be using what remains to him much more powerfully than most people do. A man who doesn't have the use of his legs might be congratulated on the biceps he's built up to enable himself to get around in a wheelchair, and a man who can't speak loudly might be congratulated on his ability to get his point across with admirable force regardless. You can talk about masculine role models and identify characteristics they have in common.

What makes a woman?

Living with a disability, especially if one has inadequate care provision or has a carer who doesn't respect one's gender, can make it difficult to maintain high standards of personal care. This can be a major concern for trans women who feel that, as a result, they will be unable to achieve feminine beauty norms. To an extent, it's a problem that can be resolved – electrolysis to remove facial hair can do away with the need to shave (even if it takes several sessions to achieve it) and taking oestrogen naturally softens the skin. If these things are options for the individual concerned, they can provide some reassurance.

The hormones that are often taken as part of transition cause body fat to be redistributed, which has positive effects, changing the overall shape of the body, but can also increase the tendency for trans women to put on weight if they struggle to get enough exercise due to disability or illness. This can make it difficult for them to meet the beauty standards expected of women in our society. While this can be a cause of stress for any women, it's additionally complicated for trans women by the fact that any deviation from feminine beauty norms can be associated with failure to be a 'real woman'.

Undermining trans women's confidence in relation to their appearance is a common tactic for people who are hostile to them because they are trans. It's further problematic because trans women who have transitioned later in life don't have as much social preparation for dealing with misogyny as other women do, and can therefore find things upsetting when others have learned to brush them off. On the plus side, if they are happy to talk about the way they experience misogyny, they can help service providers identify problems that may have been allowed to fester for too long because other women are less inclined to complain about them.

Some women argue that trans women can never be 'real women' because they don't share all the same experiences when growing up. Of course, cis girls who grow up with disabilities often don't share all those experiences either. What disabled and trans people almost always share with cis women is the experience of being treated as socially inferior and the experience of having to be wary of male aggression.

Non-binary experiences of gender and disability

When you're working with a non-binary person, it's important not to assume that you know which characteristics will be important to them in expressing their gender (or lack of gender), as this can vary a great deal. Don't try to reassure them by complimenting characteristics that are heavily gendered by society – such as a slender figure or strong arms – unless you have already established that these are things they feel positive about.

Some non-binary people experience dysphoria associated with disability because it makes it difficult for them to live up to a societal idea of what androgyny looks like, often described as 'masculinity lite', tall and thin. You can help by showing them that you respect who they are and don't need such cues to remind you of that. It won't usually make the dysphoria go away but it can help to reassure them that there's a place for them in society. It can also help to remind them that society is changing and becoming more aware of non-binary identities, so if they have to deal with people being sceptical about their gender because of the way they look, that might get better in the future.

Other non-binary people say that they feel they're actually more likely to be correctly gendered if they're disabled, but not for positive reasons. People with disabilities are often treated as if they don't have any kind of sexuality and, by the same token, they can be treated as if they have no place on the gender spectrum. This is a form of objectification – disabled people are not always recognised as fully human. Although non-binary people may find it a relief not to be associated with conventional expectations of men or women, they want their humanity to be recognised, just like anyone else.

Safety concerns

There is another major issue that concerns chronically ill and disabled people who are trans, which can discourage some from coming out, let alone transitioning: personal safety. It's a sad fact that trans people are significantly more likely to be physically or sexually assaulted than members of the population at large, and if they are physically unable to run away or adequately defend themselves, this can be a much more frightening prospect.

Although transphobic aggression is less common when trans people are in the company of cis adults, carers need to be aware that it's something they could encounter when out and about with a trans person they are supporting. If this happens, it's best to take a lead from the trans person, who may know the aggressor(s) and have a better sense of how to handle the situation. Always be ready to call the police if you think that you or the cared-for person are at risk. Make a note of the time and date of the incident and any details you remember about it afterwards. In the case of ongoing harassment, it's a good idea to keep a diary of incidents. This will help the police, whether your client chooses to contact them immediately or chooses not to but later changes their mind.

Learning disorders and competence

People who have learning disorders are just as likely to be trans as anybody else (in fact, in some cases there is believed to be an increased chance of them identifying as trans because they may not fully comprehend the stigma associated with it so they won't talk themselves out of it). Because being trans is often seen as the product of a decision rather than as a simple state of being, however, they may encounter additional barriers to acceptance.

Family members or health and care providers may consider them to be incompetent to recognise their gender (or understand the social consequences of expressing it), even in circumstances where they consider them competent in regard to other matters. This mirrors the way in which, as disability rights campaigners have pointed out, such people are often perceived as lacking competence in regard to their sexuality.[38]

In a situation where it is not possible to determine that an individual understands the issues well enough to consent to hormone treatment or surgery, there is still the option of a social transition like that available to young children, whereby a new name and pronouns are used and a new style of presentation adopted. With the right support from family members and support services, this can be a highly positive experience and go a long way towards reducing any dysphoria that the person concerned is feeling. Even if it turns out not to be something that they want to persist with after giving it a try, it's easy enough to reverse, no harm is done and it can sometimes improve their understanding of social relations. It's important not to let the social anxieties of care providers complicate what is ultimately a harmless process of exploration.

For some people who are quite severely affected by learning disorders, it can still be possible to understand issues around gender and transition as long as enough time is taken in doing so. Achieving a deep understanding of a major issue by studying it and thinking about it over time can be well within the competence of individuals who struggle to process information quickly enough to keep up with others when discussing minor issues.

Individuals in this situation should be assessed on a case-by-case basis. It should not be assumed either that it is impossible for them to be trans or that it is impossible for them to understand what transition means.

See Chapter 7 on sensory impairments and disability for more detail on these issues.

Power of attorney

Elderly trans people and those who suffer from illnesses that place them at significant risk of brain injury – for example, due to a stroke or a fit – should be encouraged to think about power of attorney. Legally granting this power – should it be needed – to a person whom they trust to respect their gender means that they are protected from any attempts to challenge the way they present themselves and live their lives. Such attempts are, sadly, all too common in situations where relatives disapprove of an individual's transition.

In addition to granting power of attorney, it's a good idea for trans people to make what is known as an advance statement – essentially a guide to how they would prefer to be treated when they are no longer able to make their wishes known. Although this lacks legal force, it can be very helpful to care providers. It can cover matters such as preferred presentation (everything from personal grooming to clothing), name and pronoun preferences, and what is or is not acceptable to disclose to others in different sets of circumstances.

4

The Transition Process

Many trans people seek medical assistance to aid in their transition. This may involve psychiatric assessment, hormone treatment or surgical procedures, although not all trans people choose to go through each of these stages. Different NHS protocols are in operation in different parts of the UK. Some people choose to use private healthcare companies for all or part of their transition, while other people may arrive in the UK as visitors or immigrants having already received some treatments not normally offered here, and seeking additional medical support.

Transition as a process

Regardless of how other people may see it, most trans people don't regard transition as one pivotal moment, whether that's the time spent having genital surgery or the day when a gender recognition certificate arrives. Instead, they see it as a process with several different elements. These are likely to include the following:

- **Exploring gender.** Now that society is more open about gender variance, this is increasingly likely to take place early in life and be part of the process of growing up. For some people, however, it is repressed for a long time, or simply doesn't occur until later in life.

- **Deciding what fits.** For some people, this is very clear. For others, it may be necessary to experiment with different ways of expressing identity before knowing how to present it to the wider world. Some people remain in flux and are comfortable that way.

- **Coming out.** Sooner or later, most people decide it's time to talk about how they feel. Who they talk to first will depend on who they feel close to and who they expect to be sympathetic. Some people take a while to build up the courage to tell those they love.

- **Changing presentation.** Most people try to communicate their gender through things like clothing choices, hairstyle, make-up (or lack thereof) and behaviour. They may also start asking people to use different pronouns and titles for them at this point.

- **Considering hormones.** Not everyone feels that hormones are right for them and in some cases there are medical impediments to taking them, but for many trans people they are life-changing, easing dysphoria and changing the body so it begins to look and feel right.

- **Considering surgery.** Not everyone wants surgery and it's not medically advisable for everyone; but where it is wanted, it can do a lot to ease dysphoria, and many trans people feel that it's the final step in freeing them up to live authentic lives.

It's important to note that not all trans people take all these steps and some go through them in a different order. There is no one true way to be trans. People can feel complete and satisfied with their lives at different stages. Some people experience transition as a journey that never really stops (just as, for instance, a cis woman might discover different ways of relating to her femininity as she goes through different stages of life and people's perceptions of her change). For others, it's a journey with a definite end point – some people feel that after they have undergone the surgeries they want, they no longer have trans identities and simply wish to get on with their lives as men or women, putting the past behind them.

For people who are disabled or have chronic illnesses, some of the above-mentioned steps may be difficult or even impossible. You should never assume that somebody in this position who has not changed their presentation, taken hormones or had surgery doesn't *want* to. Even coming out can be difficult for people whose care needs mean that they are much more dependent on the approval of others than most people are. As a consequence of this, they are more likely to be 'invisible' in their transness – sure of who they are but less able to express it.

When a trans person first comes out

Coming out as trans is a difficult process. Trans people may spend years building up to it. They may be very frightened about what could happen if you don't approve, especially if they are already dependent on you for care in relation to a disability or chronic illness. This means that it's essential that your initial response is supportive, even if you're not very sure how you can help.

Many trans people thoroughly research medical transition pathways before coming out, so you should not assume that they don't know what they're getting into or that they need more time to think about it. Be honest about your limitations but answer their questions as best you can.

Bear in mind that many people choose a healthcare professional as the very first person they come out to, before any of their loved ones. This can be a highly emotional moment. Take your time and try to calm them down before the appointment ends. If they're shaking badly, you may need to advise them to rest for a while before driving home. Reassure them that your discussion will remain confidential.

People who are not neurotypical may need additional advice and support to deal with the coming-out process. Some people in this situation struggle to understand social conventions around gender and so fail to anticipate situations in which they may be met with hostility. Others instinctively assume that if they feel happy about being trans, then those close to them will also feel happy about it, and they will need both to be prepared for possible disappointment and to be advised on how they might broach the subject gently.

When you are helping a trans person in this situation, it's a good idea to refer them to a local trans support group.

Children who come out as trans should be advised about the available options both in the immediate term and in the future, and reassured that they can expect support from medical and care services no matter what they choose to do. Unless and until they request a referral to a gender identity clinic or expressly agree to bringing their parents (or guardians) into the discussion, the matter should remain confidential. Outing children to their parents can place them at risk even in situations where there is no obvious sign of problems within the family. If you are worried that the child may be self-harming or at risk of attempting suicide because of dysphoria, raise it as a general mental health concern rather than discussing issues around gender.

Sadly, some trans people do not get appropriate support from their GPs. In fact, poor GP management of trans-related issues is the most common cause of complaint by trans people about medical services in the UK.[39] Many people report that their GPs simply refuse to deal with them, saying that they don't know enough about trans issues, that they don't believe being trans is a real thing, or that they don't believe those particular individuals are trans. Some refuse to prescribe oestrogen or testosterone even when it has been recommended by a specialist, and some agree to do so but worry about it so much that they refuse to put it on repeat prescription. Although there are circumstances in which, due to coexisting health issues, close monitoring is important, requiring an appointment for each prescription is highly problematic given the workloads many GP surgeries currently face. Trans people can be faced with a situation in which they need monthly appointments but waiting lists for appointments are more than a month long, leading to them either buying hormones on the black market (with all the attendant risks) or having breaks in medication, which can also be dangerous. By trying to provide extra protection for their patients, these GPs can actually place them at risk.

More disturbingly, some GPs insist on examining the genitals of trans people before prescribing hormones, something that is not medically necessary in the absence of disease, and still less so if the patient is under the care of a gender identity clinic or attending a well man or well woman clinic. Afraid of losing their access to hormones, trans patients can feel unable to assert themselves in such situations and unable to say no. This places them in an extremely vulnerable situation.

Like other patients, trans people are often unaware that they have the option of changing GPs, or don't know how to do so. Others report that they have had to do so three or four times before finding ones who were prepared to treat them and would interact with them respectfully. General Medical Council *Good Medical Practice* guidelines state that doctors who have a conscientious objection to a particular procedure have an overriding duty to explain that to patients, tell them that they have the right to see another doctor and give them enough information to exercise that right. Likewise, they must not allow their personal views to affect the treatment they provide or arrange.[40] Sadly, this is not always what trans people experience in practice.

The early stages

The first steps in transition are psychological and social. Most trans people make changes to their appearance at home before they feel ready to do so in public. This may mean that they need help to change their appearance before and after venturing outside. They may adopt a new name for use at home but not immediately be ready to use it with everyone. If you are supporting someone in this position as a carer, you will need to be very careful not to use the new name – or new pronouns – in any situation where the trans person may not be ready for it. Using it in private, however, is an important affirmative step and will help to give the trans person confidence in your support. This will help with every day-to-day interaction in which trust is needed, whether or not it has anything directly to do with gender.

When a trans person feels ready to start hormone treatment, GPs have the option of prescribing directly. Alternatively, they may make a referral to a gender identity clinic where specialist support can be provided – something that will have to be done sooner or later anyway if the patient is contemplating a surgical transition on the NHS. GPs should be aware that waiting lists for such clinics can be lengthy,[41] so they should consider the patient's needs carefully before deciding whether or not to provide hormones in the meantime.

It is never appropriate for a GP to refuse to refer a patient to a gender identity clinic simply because they don't believe that patient is trans, any more than it would be appropriate to refuse to refer a patient who reported cardiac problems to a specialist simply because their pulse was steady when they visited the surgery. Sadly, this happens all too often. Trans people report being told, among other things, that they are taking money away from cancer patients. Some GPs erroneously believe that a mental health assessment is needed, which is not true either for a referral or for a hormone prescription, and which is likely to lead to further confusion because most mental health professionals do not have the expertise to assess transition-related needs (that's what gender identity clinics are *for*). Others believe that local funding has to be arranged, which has not been the case in England since 2013.

For patients attending a gender identity clinic, the appointments system can be very taxing. Travel can be exhausting for disabled people, and staying in a hotel is more expensive if one needs to stay in an adapted room because this makes it harder to take advantage of the discounts available to other people. Taking along a carer adds to the cost yet again. Service users report that it's all too easy to be discharged if health problems or difficulties with travel lead to missed appointments. There is a policy to the effect that patients should not advance along the treatment pathway if they are psychologically unstable, but this doesn't distinguish very well between ongoing problems and temporary instability, such as that which might be experienced as an immediate consequence of being assaulted or being bereaved.

Concern has been expressed that the treatment offered by gender identity clinics is neither consistent nor transparent, and that in some cases it may involve questioning of dubious relevance.[42] Patients have been asked if they have gay relatives, what video games they play, what kind of toys they played with as children, their choice of books and television programmes, and even how they tie their shoelaces. They have been subjected to intensive questioning about their sex lives and masturbatory habits, even in front of accompanying parents. They have been subject to assumptions based on how they sit and how they speak (despite the fact that they may well have trained themselves out of behaviour that sends a gender signal which clashes with their presentation, for safety reasons). They may also be classified using old-fashioned terminology that doesn't accurately reflect their identities. Patients who are afraid that they may be denied access to hormones or surgery often feel unable to challenge these things.

Despite all this, many patients find that attending a gender identity clinic is helpful in its own right. For some, it's the first time they have felt accepted in their gender by somebody who really understands where they are coming from.

Hormone treatment and fertility

Before prescribing hormones, it's advisable to discuss the issue of fertility. Some trans people may want to store sperm or eggs so that they can retain the option of having their own biological children. Although in most cases it's possible to pause hormone treatment after a few months and let the body readjust in order to retrieve sperm or eggs, this can be more traumatic than waiting and taking care of it before starting. Storing sperm is a quick and easy process, so this is straightforward for trans women. In contrast, the process of producing enough eggs for storage can itself make dysphoria worse in trans men because of the effects of the hormones involved and because of the swelling it creates in the body, which temporarily enhances a typically feminine body shape.

Some doctors overlook the significance of fertility to people with significant physical impairments, often assuming that they would not want to have children or simply that they don't have sex lives or serious romantic relationships. Others assume that trans people's long-term relationships will end when they transition, because they don't recognise that some people are bisexual or that straight or gay people can find ways to work around the usual limits of their sexuality for the sake of maintaining intimacy with someone they love. Or, indeed, that many couples find that love is enough to keep them together even if their sexual intimacy comes to an end.

An increasing number of trans men are choosing to pause testosterone treatment in order to become pregnant, even some years after their initial transition. The desire to become pregnant does not reflect a desire to detransition or be perceived as female. It can happen when a trans man is in a relationship with a cis man and they want children; when he is in a relationship with a woman and she is not able to conceive or carry a pregnancy to term; or for various other reasons, including the simple personal wish to carry a child (which a not insignificant number of cis men also experience). No evidence has been found to date to suggest that gestating in the body of a trans man is harmful to a child. There is, however, no guarantee that a trans man attempting to become pregnant in this manner will succeed.

Hormonal transition – trans men

The changes that occur when a trans man starts taking testosterone can be quite sudden, and they may mean that he needs different kinds of support. They don't happen in the same order for everybody and some of them may not happen at all – patterns of hair growth, for instance, are heavily influenced by genetic factors as well as hormones. Nevertheless, it's a good idea to be ready for the following:

- **Muscle gain.** This occurs mostly in the upper body. In some cases, it can be liberating for disabled trans men, compensating for other difficulties and enabling them to live more independently. If they still need to be lifted around, however, you will need to be prepared for them to weigh more, and it may be time to think about using assistive devices even if you have managed before.

- **Beard growth.** This usually means that shaving or trimming a beard becomes necessary for the first time. Some disabled people will need help with this.

- **Hair loss.** This can be distressing for trans men as it often is for cis men, and support may be needed to find new ways of managing personal grooming in order to minimise its impact.

- **Acne.** Because transition is a lot like puberty, it includes the unfortunate side effects of puberty. Acne can be particularly painful for disabled people who struggle to change position, especially if the back is affected, so consideration will need to be given to support options when the affected person is sitting or lying down. Dressings and pain relief may be needed where they would not be as important to a person with more mobility.

- **Voice changes.** Although the process is not usually as dramatic as it is for young cis men, trans men usually do experience their voices breaking, and they may lose their voices entirely for a short period of time. This can be problematic in situations where they usually provide a lot of moment-by-moment direction to carers. If possible, alternative systems of communication should be worked out ahead of time, just in case.

Carers should also be prepared for trans men to become more confident, which is usually a positive thing but can sometimes overstep the line into aggression. Like young cis men, they need to learn by experience how to recognise and curtail this, but as adults they can usually do so more quickly and the hormonal effect on mood tends to diminish anyway as their bodies get used to a higher base level of testosterone.

Testosterone is normally administered by intramuscular injection every two to three months. Towards the end of this cycle, some trans men find that they become lethargic and struggle to think clearly. They may need additional help with things they can normally manage independently. As a carer, it's a good idea to keep track of this cycle so that you know when to expect such problems, especially if there are additional health issues present.

Hormonal transition – trans women

Just like trans men, trans women have diverse experiences of hormonal transition and don't all go through the same changes. It's worth being alert to the following likely changes, however, so that you can provide support as needed:

- **Weight gain.** Although most trans women lose muscle to the point where they carry about the same amount as cis women, this process can take several months. Water retention can happen in a matter of weeks. As fat is redistributed around the body, the dynamics of balance change, which can be a problem for disabled people if they already have difficulty walking or otherwise moving around. It means that carers who are used to lifting them may suddenly find that they need to do so differently. It's also common for trans women to gain extra body fat in the first few months after starting to take hormones. If this is a health concern, a fresh physiotherapy programme may be needed to help manage it.

- **Breast development.** Most trans women experience some natural breast growth when they start hormone treatment, although on average it's not as substantial as in cis women. Just like young cis women going through this, they often find that the new breast tissue is tender. It can be easily bruised and can also be hurt by tight clothing or clothing that rubs. Carers will need to be aware of this if moving or dressing a disabled person, and may also need to help with the purchase of more suitable clothes. Most major high street clothing stores are happy to fit bras for trans women and will do so without any prejudice or fuss.

- **Eczema.** Just as trans men's skin tends to become more oily with testosterone, trans women's skin tends to become drier with oestrogen, and this means that eczema is a common problem. It's particularly uncomfortable for disabled people who are not able to reach areas of affected skin (where they can, tapping is a much better remedy than scratching). The best preventative treatment is a simple moisturiser, and help from a carer may be needed to apply this. If eczema persists, a GP can also prescribe topical treatments to bring a flare under control.

- **Heightened emotions.** When first taking hormones, most trans women report that they find themselves experiencing enhanced emotional sensitivity and a sense that they have a deeper emotional connection with the world around them. This can be highly positive in some respects but it can also be disorientating. Until they have adjusted, they may find themselves getting very upset over little things that would not previously have bothered them. This can be particularly problematic if they frequently have to deal with transphobia or the stresses associated with a disability or illness. Carers need to be ready to show extra sensitivity themselves, but should also remember not to take it personally if they become the targets of unhappy outbursts – a little patience will allow room for any significant concerns to be discussed more calmly.

Once the initial changes have settled down, trans women who have had their testes removed have a fairly stable hormone cycle much like a cis woman's, so although they can experience changes of mood, these will not usually seem out of the ordinary to carers. If they have not had their testes removed, however, they will need to take anti-androgens. These can result in a more dramatic cycle, with some trans women feeling acutely depressed in the last few days before their next anti-androgen injection is due.

Young trans people

When prepubertal children identify as trans, there is normally no need for medical intervention beyond referral to a gender identity clinic. Once puberty begins, however, puberty blockers are recommended. These allow children to grow up without drastic changes taking place in their bodies, until they reach an age where they are competent to understand the implications of cross-sex hormone treatment, which is not provided to adolescents on the NHS unless they have taken puberty blockers for at least one year first. The principle of Gillick competence[43] could be applied here, but within the NHS this is not the case and no cross-sex hormones are prescribed below the age of 16. The Endocrine Society argues, however, that cross-sex hormone treatment at an earlier age can sometimes be appropriate, and in 2018 a private practitioner was cleared of wrongdoing when she prescribed cross-sex hormones to a 12-year-old patient.[44]

It is worth noting that testosterone and oestrogen are both used to treat young intersex people below the age of 16, and that oestrogen is available to cis women under 16 in contraceptive pills.

Puberty blockers affect bone mineralisation, with the effect becoming more pronounced when they are used for extended periods. They are rarely used in young trans people for more than five years and bone health is monitored closely throughout. Remineralisation normally occurs within the first year after treatment is stopped and the young person either chooses to go through the puberty typical for someone of their birth-assigned gender or receives treatment with cross-sex hormones, inducing a different pubertal process.

When talking to young people, it's important to be aware that they may be uncomfortable discussing some issues in front of their parents. If their parents are also their carers, they may be used to being there all the time, but GPs and specialists should encourage them to leave the room for short periods, if the young person is comfortable with that, to give the young person the opportunity to raise any issues that might otherwise be overlooked. Furthermore, decisions should never be made in conversation with the parents without the young person being present and invited to participate.

Listening to young people is important. Sadly, some report that they don't feel they are taken seriously by doctors when they talk about gender, even if they have had consistent feelings about it for several years. Some say that they have been told by doctors that they're just confused about their sexuality, or about the sexuality of parents who happen to be lesbian, gay or bisexual, or even that they are trying to get attention because they resent their parents for divorcing. While it's true that young people can be naive and they can be rebellious, this doesn't mean that they can't be genuinely trans.

At present, young people who age out of these treatment protocols are asked to wait – sometimes for over a year – before being reassessed as adult patients. This is obviously problematic and has been subject to extensive criticism. It also contributes to a situation whereby people who have identified as trans from early childhood and have attended a gender identity clinic for years, but have not enjoyed the family or school support necessary to start living in their preferred gender role and so cannot begin the real-life experience test until they reach adulthood, may be well into their 20s before they are eligible for surgery on the NHS.

Non-binary people

Where they can get medical support to transition, non-binary people already go through non-standard care pathways because their needs are more varied than those of binary trans people. Having to work around a disability or illness adds an additional layer of complexity. This can make it more difficult for people in that position to feel confident about the transition process and seek help as soon as they should, a problem compounded by the fact that they can face multiple barriers to support services. Not only are trans support groups sometimes unable to accommodate the access needs of disabled people, but some are focused on binary trans people to the extent that non-binary people can feel unwelcome.

In addition to this, service providers often find it more difficult to support people who face complex issues and require additional problem-solving efforts on their part. It is very helpful if service providers can minimise the number of individuals they have to deal with, so that they don't have to keep explaining their circumstances over and over again. Care pathways should be plotted out in advance as far as possible, so that it's easy for the different professionals involved to see what is required of them and coordinate with each other.

Heart health

Cardiac problems can make it risky for trans people to take oestrogen or testosterone. In this situation, doctors and patients need to work together to find the best way forward. Doctors should be aware that if a trans person is determined to take hormones regardless of the advice given, they are relatively easy to obtain on the black market,[45] especially for trans women. Since risks can be higher if a patient's use of hormones is unsupervised and no further measures can be taken to tackle related problems (e.g. by providing hypotensives), a harm-reduction approach needs to be taken.

Stopping hormone treatment should not be treated as an easy answer, because for trans people with severe dysphoria it can lead to very bad mental health outcomes, which can themselves increase the risk of premature death. Where the risk of cardiac problems is severe, however, some trans people still decide that it's the right option for them. Should they do so, it's important that they are given the right support and that the decision is not conflated with a desire to stop transitioning. Some trans people still go on to live fulfilling lives in the gender roles that feel right for them without taking hormones, and a successful social transition potentially helps to alleviate dysphoria even in the absence of any medical treatment.

In some cases, cardiac problems also rule out surgery or add an additional element of risk to it. This is something that is gradually changing, partly due to advances in anaesthetic technology and partly due to refinements in surgical technique. Top surgery for trans men, in particular, can now be carried out much less intrusively and more quickly than was the case a decade ago, reducing the need for prolonged anaesthetic use and reducing the overall strain on the body.

Detransition

No exploration of the subject of transition is complete without considering detransition. This refers to the decision some people make to reverse the transition process and return to their original gender roles.

Rates of regret over surgical transition are astonishingly low compared with regret rates for other forms of elective surgery, with most studies finding them to be between 2% and 4%.[46] Furthermore, regret rates have declined over time as surgical techniques have improved and the rate of major complications occurring has declined.

Individual regret also appears to decrease over time. This may be because, initially, some of those treated are unhappy that the results are not as good as they had hoped for. Others may put too much focus on transition as a means of solving all the problems they have in life and ending all their sorrows, only to discover that it falls short of this, and they then need time to appreciate the positive things that it *has* done for them.

For some individuals, however, transitioning doesn't work out. These people fall into three main groups. The first comprises people who find the social burden of transition too great to bear. The second comprises people who were going through a process of exploring gender and had no other means of finding out what was right for them. The third comprises people who appear to have been misdiagnosed as trans in the first place.

The first group includes people who try to retreat from transition after experiencing family breakdown, feeling that they are forced to choose between living in an authentic gender role and being with the people they love. It also includes people who face more public hostility than they feel able to cope with, and people who are situationally vulnerable to hostility, such as people going into prison. A shortage of employment opportunities may also be a factor. It's notable that people who have transitioned to live as men are far less likely to detransition than people who have transitioned to live as women – the former group blend in much more easily than the latter and are significantly less likely to be identified as trans by strangers. In addition to this, trans men don't have the sudden experience of having to deal with sexism and misogyny, which can feel overwhelming for some trans women.

Because detransition makes for sensational headlines, some of what is represented that way in the media is in fact a simple case of delayed or interrupted treatment. When she initially transitioned at the age of 18, Ria Cooper was hailed as 'Britain's youngest transexual' and her story featured extensively in the media. As a result, she received a huge amount of attention from the public, much of it hostile,[47] and she simply wasn't equipped to deal with it. Unable to find a job, she turned to escorting and was attacked by a client, which led to a nervous breakdown. Her consequent inability to attend gender clinic appointments or access hormones led to headlines announcing that she was detransitioning. Finally, some years later, came a cluster of headlines announcing that she was going through a third 'gender swap'. In fact, Ria felt consistently female throughout.

People in the second group may take some time to realise their regret, because exploring life in a different gender role is part of the journey through which they discover what actually works best for them. They may go on to adopt non-binary identities or to carve out social space for themselves as feminine men or masculine women. This group includes people who say that at the time of transitioning they had little awareness of the range of gender options available to them and believed that going through a binary transition was the only alternative to living as they were – something that appears to be decreasing as public awareness of gender diversity increases. It also includes people who didn't trust their doctors and felt that a binary transition including genital surgery was the only option being offered, so they would have to go through with part of it and then 'revert' in order to get to the point where they actually wanted to be all along.

Some people in this group say that they don't actually regret the experience of having transitioned, but they just don't feel that the body it has given them is – or continues to be – right for them. Some may live for years or even decades in the gender role they transitioned to, only to decide that they have reached a point in their lives where they feel they can live more happily in their original role.

The third group includes a comparatively high proportion of people who have elected to transition privately, without first going through the counselling that is required before access to surgery is available on the NHS. In some cases, individuals have undertaken that counselling and been discouraged from transitioning only to pursue it through a private route. Detailed research in this area is sparse but it would appear that mental illness can play a role.

A small number of people detransition after arriving at a religious or ideological standpoint that persuades them that living in a gender role different to the one they were assigned at birth is wrong. One woman who briefly returned to living as a man reported that she had felt very isolated because of her disability and that she was persuaded to detransition by a group of women who made her feel welcomed and supported. She subsequently retransitioned and was sad to discover that her new friends melted away. Her case illustrates how vulnerable disabled trans people, in particular, can be to peer pressure.

Supporting detransitioners

Some detransitioners simply stop communicating with doctors and are impossible to reach. Where this is not the case, appropriate support needs to be given.

People who are contemplating detransition but are uncertain about the best way forward should be offered counselling to help them clarify their thoughts. Mental illness may be a factor in creating feelings of dissatisfaction or hopelessness, in which case – just as with people considering transition for the first time – they should be encouraged to explore treatment options before making potentially life-changing decisions. They should also be monitored to ensure that mental illness does not develop as a result of hormonal or social changes associated with detransition.

Where a patient is determined to stop taking hormones – the most common step in detransition – they should be supported in coming off them safely. If they have had their ovaries or testes removed, they should be advised about the risks associated with having very low levels of both oestrogen and testosterone, and offered the opportunity to take artificial hormones of the type their bodies originally produced.

Some people lose a lot of friends when they detransition, and they may also lose the support of a wider community that has become an important part of their social support structure. Other trans people may consider them traitors, or they may internalise these feelings. Others may politicise their stories to attack the idea of transition, even if they don't feel that's at all appropriate. Because issues around transition and detransition are highly politicised, it can be hard to make room for personal feelings. As always, anything that impacts social support tends to be additionally problematic for trans people who also have disabilities.

It's important to help people understand that even if the decision to transition was wrong for them, that doesn't mean that they could have made a better decision at the time, with the information that they had available to them. Transition and detransition do not need to be seen as indicative of failure, but can be looked at positively as part of a journey that increases wisdom and understanding of the self.

Detransitioners will need to be aware that 'reverse' genital surgery is not likely to be as successful as their original surgery because there will be less tissue to work with. Chest surgery tends to be less problematic in this regard but can still involve additional difficulties. Trans men who are detransitioning will need to undergo treatment to remove facial hair and will not recover hair lost to male pattern baldness, although hair transplants can go some way towards creating a more typically feminine appearance.

Detransitioners who feel a strong need to revert to their original gender roles may worry about getting stuck in a gender-ambiguous position, especially in light of the limitations of surgical options. They will often need support to deal with this. Although every individual's needs are different, it can be worth noting that many detransitioners find they are able to live comfortably after a partial reversal of treatment, even without further surgery, especially if they are easily able to 'pass' in their original gender role.

Some people choose to detransition without surgery because they believe that altering the body is wrong in itself and that they should never have done it the first time.

Retransition

One reason for encouraging detransitioners to go through counselling and avoid rushing into further surgery is that many go on to retransition again in the future. This is rarely a case of a complete reversal of gender feelings followed by a second complete reversal. Most often, it occurs when detransition was prompted by external factors and wasn't really right for them.

Retransition can be as simple as starting to take hormones again, changing aspects of gender presentation and reverting to the name and pronouns used after the original transition. In some cases, retransitioners choose a new name in recognition of the fact that this is a new stage of their lives. This can also help them to distance themselves from the initial process of transition and detransition, which often has a lot of negative feelings associated with it.

5

Surgical Transition

Not every trans person chooses to or is able to have surgery, but for many this is the primary goal. Understanding what it involves can help disabled people and those providing support to work out what could and could not be possible for them, and what might be necessary to make surgical goals more accessible. In some cases, alternative surgeries are available if the first-choice surgeries entail too many medical or practical problems.

Understanding surgical transition will also give carers a better understanding of some of the long-term issues trans people commonly face. This can help them to work around pain or heightened sensitivity more effectively, providing a better experience for their clients.

Eligibility for surgery

Whether they are seeking NHS-based or private treatment, disabled and chronically ill people face additional barriers in proving their eligibility for surgery. Because all the procedures involved in transition are considered to be elective surgery (although some individual practitioners describe them as essential and life-saving), surgeons are reluctant to take on anyone they think faces a significantly elevated risk of developing complications during surgery. When accessing treatments in the private sector, it's necessary to factor in (a) whether or not the work will take place in a hospital with full emergency facilities, and (b) what the additional cost will be if complications occur. Insurance can be used to control the latter but it can again increase the overall cost or increase reluctance on the part of the surgeon.

Although the Equality Act requires UK plastic surgery clinics to make reasonable adjustments for disabled patients, such adjustments cannot always be guaranteed in clinics in other countries, and this means that simple issues such as needing to be lifted rather than rolled when transferring between beds can make it impossible for disabled people to access treatment there. Even in the UK, disabled people may need to go through a lengthy process of negotiation in order to be sure that their basic needs can be met before they go in for treatment.

Most surgeons and NHS trusts have a requirement that trans people go through one to two years of what is termed *real-life experience* in the gender role they are transitioning to before they are eligible for surgery. Although the most recent WPATH guidelines on this are fairly flexible about what it should involve, there is still an expectation that people will be in education, work or training during this period, in order to demonstrate that they can function within society. Some clinics have quite old-fashioned ideas about what living as a man or living as a woman involves. There is very little consistency in what is asked of non-binary people who feel the need to have surgery.

Disabled trans people frequently report problems with this. They may not be able to work, study or train. They may not be able to afford to study or find an employer who will take them on, or successfully hold on to a job, due to disability discrimination.[48] Some even report having their access to hormone treatment stopped due to this, because they are seen as failing to demonstrate adequate commitment to transition.

Service providers should take into account the need for reasonable adjustment when requiring disabled people to go through the real-life experience process. Where the intent is to demonstrate the ability to function in society, for instance, regularly undertaking social activities or volunteering (often possible where working is not because it tends to be more flexible and involve fewer hours) can be considered as an alternative form of proof. Where disabled or chronically ill people are unable to cope with this and spend most of their time at home, and where that situation is not expected to change, providers should ask themselves why it matters whether or not that person is able to manage social contact effectively in a new gender role. In those circumstances, transition is essentially a private process.

Disabled people can also have difficulty with the real-life experience process because they are at higher risk than the average trans person when it comes to prejudice and discrimination, and often feel less able to escape hostile situations or defend themselves. This should not be taken as a reason to deny treatment. Because it usually takes place early on in the transition process, real-life experience makes trans people particularly vulnerable. At this stage, they are unlikely to have undergone the physical changes needed to 'pass' in the new gender role, or to have acquired the vocal techniques, mannerisms and so forth which they have a good chance of acquiring later. For this reason, the experience of transphobia tends to be worse during this period than it is post-transition, and struggling to cope with the level of transphobia experienced at this point does not necessarily indicate that an individual will be unable to cope with it post-transition.

Obesity

The single most common health concern affecting the provision of surgery for trans people is obesity. This is a particular issue when it comes to genital surgery because of the length of time for which the patient needs to be under anaesthetic. Consequently, it's often necessary to delay surgery until the patient is able to lose weight.

Losing weight is particularly difficult for people with limited mobility or other health problems such as diabetes. Trans people in this situation can benefit from additional support from a dietician or physiotherapist, but may find it difficult to access these services because the process of transition is not always recognised as a priority.

For trans people already suffering from depression or anxiety associated with dysphoria, the stress of delaying surgery can create a vicious circle, leading to decreased activity levels or comfort eating. In other cases, however, having surgery as a goal helps with weight loss.

Surgical options

Despite the popular belief that gender reassignment surgery is a magical process, in which an individual goes in looking like a typical member of one sex and comes out looking like a typical member of another, the reality is more complex. There are in fact several different types of surgery that trans people may go through in order to achieve their desired results. These include, but are not limited to, the following:

Removal of the testes

Often carried out separately from other genital modification procedures, this process, also known as an orchiectomy, is a fairly simple operation, taking less than an hour, and it can be an option even for those whose health problems make prolonged anaesthesia unwise. It has dramatic effects on the body, significantly reducing the amount of testosterone naturally present in the system, so that hormone treatment doses can usually be reduced by a significant amount. This in turn reduces the risk of long-term complications such as the formation of blood clots.

Because patients can normally go home on the same day, orchiectomy is an option even for those whose care requirements make it difficult for them to stay overnight in hospital.

An orchiectomy can be performed with or without removal of the scrotal sac. Although many trans women find the presence of the scrotum unpleasant, keeping it in place means that there is more skin available to use if a vaginoplasty is undertaken in the future.

Patients who would like to retain the option of having their own biological children in future should arrange to store sperm before this procedure is carried out.

Removal of the penis and construction of a vagina

Although they are technically two procedures (penectomy and vaginoplasty), these operations are usually carried out together, as this enables tissue from the penis to be used in constructing a vagina. If the testes have not previously been removed, they are usually removed at this point. If the scrotal sac has not previously been removed, its skin forms the primary graft used to line the vagina. In its absence, skin grafts are usually taken from the upper thigh. Tissue from the foreskin is also an important contributor, which means that it's harder to achieve the same smoothness and aesthetic effect if the penis has been circumcised.

This is a lengthy operation with a risk of heavy bleeding and is always carried out as an inpatient procedure followed by several days' stay in hospital. Because of the prolonged anaesthesia involved, hormone medication needs to be stopped for four to six weeks beforehand, something that many trans women find difficult as it can cause temporary depression. It is vital for the patient to carry out complex and lengthy aftercare procedures in order to get good results and prevent the new vagina from closing again.

Even with good aftercare, complications can still occur. In the past, doctors routinely assumed that all trans women were attracted to men and often believed that the whole point of vaginal construction was to be able to be vaginally penetrated by male partners. Even today, lesbian trans women who develop complications after surgery report that doctors sometimes blame it on their sexuality (incorrectly assuming that lesbian sex is never penetrative). Lesbian and asexual trans women and those who are simply not in relationships are sometimes told that they *should* have sex with men in order to get better results from surgery, an approach that is extremely inappropriate. Physically disabled trans women, meanwhile, may encounter the assumption that they're not having sex (because of the myth that disabled people don't experience sexual desire or that nobody would be attracted to them) and questioning as to why, that being the case, they would want this type of surgery. In fact, most trans women say they want it for the same reason as any other aspect of physical transition – because it enables them to feel comfortable about their body.

Trans women who refer to having 'the op' are usually referring to this combined procedure.

Construction of a clitoris

The idea of constructing female genitalia without a clitoris may sound shocking to many women, but, equally, they might be unsurprised to hear that one male surgeon who practised extensively in the UK in recent decades had a reputation for describing such 'details' as 'unnecessary'. The good news for women transitioning in the UK today is that this procedure has been much improved and it is now possible to create, in most instances, a clitoris that not only looks right but offers a good level of sensitivity. Clitoroplasty is usually carried out along with vaginoplasty. It's an issue that women may wish to discuss with their doctors first, depending on the results they are looking for.

Breast enhancement

Although feminising hormone treatment usually results in breast development, the resultant tissue is usually proportionately less than in most cis women. Furthermore, trans women may prefer to have larger breasts because this balances out the shoulders and reduces their apparent size, making the shape of the body look more feminine overall.

Breast enhancement is one of the most common elective surgeries in the world, which means that those seeking it have lots of options regarding where to go, and a good deal of choice over matters such as overall breast shape. As a rule, the procedure takes one to two hours, and although it requires general anaesthetic, patients who have the operation in the morning are usually able to go home the same day. This makes it an option for people who cannot easily stay in hospital overnight due to their care requirements.

Different types of implants and different positioning techniques are available to suit different patient needs and preferences.

Hysterectomy and oophorectomy

Although it's unusual for trans men or non-binary people to feel the need to have the uterus and ovaries removed simply in order to ease gender dysphoria, doing so is recommended by some doctors in order to reduce health risks associated with transition. Specifically, it is believed to reduce the risk of endometrial cancer and ovarian cancer, both of which are thought to be more likely in people who retain those organs and take testosterone. The statistical evidence for this is fairly slight, but patients may feel that they are better safe than sorry, especially if there is a family history of one or both of these diseases.

In some cases, taking testosterone does not stop menstrual bleeding, and this can be an aggravating factor in dysphoria. Some trans men opt for these surgeries for this reason.

After the ovaries have been removed, it is usually possible to reduce the dose of testosterone required by a trans man without increasing his dysphoria. This reduces the risk of long-term complications.

Oophorectomy can be performed separately. All procedures involving hysterectomy take one to three hours and require a few days' stay in hospital followed by several weeks of restricted activity.

Creation of prosthetic testes and closure of the vagina

Scrotoplasty involves uniting the labia majora to create a scrotal sac and inserting silicone implants within it. If there is not enough labial skin available to work with, tissue expansion may be necessary beforehand.

Scrotoplasty necessitates the closing of the vaginal vault. This is the most delicate and time-consuming part of the procedure.

Because prolonged anaesthesia is needed, this is an inpatient procedure and requires a few days' hospital stay.

After surgery, a neck pillow or inflatable doughnut should be used to avoid pressure being placed on the new perineum during the healing process, which takes around three weeks.

Scrotoplasty is sometimes, but not always, carried out at the same time as the creation of a penis.

Construction of a penis

There are two options for trans men who want penises: metoidoplasty and phalloplasty. Metoidoplasty involves constructing a penis using the clitoris and phalloplasty involves constructing a penis using tissue from elsewhere on the body. As penis transplants have now been successfully carried out on cis men, it is widely expected that this will soon provide a third option for trans men.

The testosterone treatment undergone by most trans men (and some non-binary people) naturally enlarges the external part of the clitoris, and, in metoidoplasty, surgically detaching the clitoral ligaments further enhances this effect. Plastic surgery is then used to make the clitoris more closely resemble a standard penis.

It will always be comparatively small and may not be adequate for penetrative sex, but full sensation is preserved, along with natural erectile function. The aesthetic effect is usually good, with minimal scarring.

Phalloplasty, using skin from the forearm, thigh or back, results in a larger penis which some men feel looks more natural. It incorporates the tip of the clitoris to preserve sensation, although the degree of sensitivity isn't always as good as with metoidoplasty. Although a penis constructed in this manner does not become fully erect naturally, an erection can be achieved using a pump, which is sometimes concealed within a scrotoplasty.

Urethral lengthening can be used so that the urethra is extended within the body of the new penis to allow urination through the tip. Not all trans men opt for this procedure, however, as the effect is often less than perfect (spraying is a common problem) and there is a risk of complications.

A patient who is not fully satisfied with a metoidoplasty has the option of going on to have phalloplasty, but a patient who has had phalloplasty cannot subsequently have metoidoplasty.

If no scrotoplasty is carried out, it is not necessary for a person having a penis constructed to have the vagina closed. Some men prefer to leave it as it is in order to reduce the risk of surgical complications. Undergoing vaginectomy at the same time as phalloplasty, however, means that vaginal skin can be used to extend the urethra.

Many trans men choose not to undergo either phalloplasty or metoidoplasty because there is always some risk and discomfort involved and they don't feel that they are necessary for them to live their lives as men – they can use prostheses as required, and losing breasts and building muscle make a much bigger difference to being socially accepted as male. This can make them vulnerable to discrimination by carers or medical staff, however. Most people don't understand the issues around the construction of a penis so assume that all trans men have them when they have completed transition. They may refuse to accept a trans man as male if he doesn't have a penis, and put him on the wrong hospital ward or insist that he use the wrong toilets.

Removal of breasts

Breast removal is the single most sought-after surgery among trans men because it is a flat chest, rather than the appearance of the genitals, that makes the biggest difference to a man's ability to fit in socially. There are different types of breast removal surgery available which may be more or less suitable depending on the quantity of tissue that needs to be removed, the patient's feelings about scarring and whether or not keeping his nipples is a priority for him (nipple tattoos can achieve a surprisingly good aesthetic option if he decides not to keep them, and the construction of an artificial nipple is an option).

Breast removal is an inpatient procedure and usually requires a postoperative period of one to three days in hospital care. Binding continues to be necessary for around six weeks in order to support the chest during recovery. Individuals who cannot bind due to chronic health issues such as asthma will need alternative forms of support and are likely to be more restricted in their activities during the healing period.

For trans men with upper body paralysis or muscle weakness, a different approach to exercise after breast removal may be needed. Normally, regular arm movements are recommended in order to prevent stiffness. Some men may need carers to move and lift their arms for them. Others can try placing their elbows on the arms of a chair and moving the trunk of the body towards and away from each in turn. This doesn't help with muscle movement but it helps to retain flexibility.

It usually takes a few months for everything to settle down after breast removal. Some trans men experience problems with intense sensation in the nipples which makes wearing most kinds of clothing uncomfortable, but this normally declines over time. Others have issues with drainage from the site of the wound and may need further hospital treatment to resolve it, but this is a comparatively short-term issue.

Liposuction may be used at a later date in order to give the chest area more typically masculine contours.

Non-binary people with breasts often opt to have them reduced in size rather than removed entirely. This involves similar procedures but with a reduced risk of complications and reduced healing times. It can be an option for trans men who have health issues that make complete removal of the breasts a high-risk procedure.

Critics of the way trans men and non-binary people have to go through multiple psychological assessments before being given access to breast removal surgery point out that cis men suffering from gynaecomastia are usually referred directly to surgery, and argue that this represents a double standard.

Facial remodelling

All different kinds of trans people are attracted to the idea of facial remodelling designed to emphasise or reduce particular features associated with gender. As it's not available on the NHS, however, it's not seen as an option by many. Procedures vary dramatically in cost. As a rule, facial masculinisation is much cheaper than facial feminisation, and it's also easier to access, because adding implants does not, as a rule, require the same level of skill as remodelling the existing bone structure. Good facial feminisation work generally requires travel to see a specialist (those widely considered to be the best are based in Thailand), whereas basic facial masculinisation procedures are available in most major cities.

Facial masculinisation may involve lengthening the forehead and augmenting the brow; augmenting the nose, cheeks or jaw; recontouring the chin or jaw; or enhancing the appearance of the Adam's apple. There are less intrusive options involving the use of liposuction and dermal fillers which can be carried out under light sedation and may be a better choice for many people with chronic illnesses. They're usually cheaper and these days can achieve good cosmetic results, but those results don't always last for more than a few years.

Facial feminisation may involve lowering the hairline; raising the brow; changing the shape of the eye sockets; reducing the size and changing the angle of the nose; augmenting the cheeks or lips; reducing the size of the Adam's apple; or removing bone from the chin, jaw or brow. As might be expected, bone removal is the most traumatic of these procedures and can cause swelling and bruising that lasts for months. It's commonplace for women undergoing surgeries like these to have more commonplace cosmetic surgery such as a facelift carried out at the same time, minimising the overall amount of time during which the face is bruised. Older trans women sometimes say that this gives them the chance to enjoy some of the attention paid to female beauty that they missed out on in their youth.

Vocal fold surgery

One of the biggest barriers trans people face when trying to fit in socially comes not from their physical appearance but from their voice. Most trans men are able to reach at least the upper end of the typical male vocal range through exercises that change their speech habits. Many non-binary people aim for the mid range where most people find it hard to decide if a voice sounds male or female. Both of these can be harder to achieve for some disabled people. Trans women, however, struggle more than any other group. If they went through a male puberty (i.e. they didn't come out early and get access to puberty blockers), their voices will have broken, and although some still succeed in softening their voices and adopting typically feminine patterns of intonation to the extent that they're assumed to be husky-voiced cis women, for many the only thing that can make it possible to sound female is surgery.

There are several surgical options available for raising the natural pitch of the voice. Traditionally, they have all been performed through an incision in the neck, an approach that risks damage to the vocal folds and leaves some patients permanently stuck with a falsetto voice or unable to speak at all. Endoscopic surgery is now emerging as a considerably safer alternative. At the time of writing, however, it is only available in Korea and Germany, making it difficult for disabled people to access if they struggle to travel or to raise sufficient finance.

Terminology

Despite what they go through in the process of transition, trans people can be as squeamish about discussing breasts and genitals directly as anyone else. They also, as a rule, respect the squeamishness of other people. For convenience, the term *top surgery* is used to refer to all procedures involving the chest or breasts, and the term *bottom surgery* is used to refer to all procedures involving the genitals.

Familiarity with these terms is particularly useful for nurses and carers who may need to ask questions for practical reasons but want to minimise any sense of intrusiveness.

Aftercare

Aftercare can be a particular challenge for people with disabilities affecting mobility, flexibility and motor control. Partially sighted people can usually manage but may need extra support in the initial stages, along with more frequent check-ups to ensure that no problems are developing.

In some cases, the best way to provide support with aftercare is through a local practice nurse or the district nursing service.

In other cases, additional support from a kinship carer or care service provider is adequate. What is really important, however, is that an appropriate, person-centred aftercare programme is drawn up ahead of time so that any special arrangements with local service providers can be made and care provision can be made available as soon as the trans person leaves hospital.

Getting aftercare arrangements right reduces the risk of complications and the likelihood of prolonged hospital stays being required.

6

Physical Health Issues Associated with Being Transgender

Can being transgender cause health problems? Over the years, this has often been claimed to be the case, but readers should be cautious in examining these claims. Some are frequently repeated by individuals with a history of ideological hostility to trans people, and these may therefore appear to be a prominent matter of concern even though most experts consider them to lack veracity or to be only a minor concern. Others are difficult to substantiate because of the small sample sizes involved in studies. The field of transgender health is still woefully lacking in research. Nevertheless, some clear concerns emerge, most easily analysed by group.

Trans men

On current evidence, trans men face an elevated risk of the following illnesses:

- heart disease
- liver damage
- lung disease

- high blood pressure

- high cholesterol

- acne

- urethral stones.

It is critical that trans men receive the correct level of testosterone, which varies from one individual to another. Receiving too much can result in liver damage, but if this is identified early on, then it is easily resolved.

Even a healthy dose of testosterone is believed to increase the risk of heart attacks and certain types of heart disease in comparison with women. In trans men, this risk is often elevated by smoking. Trans men are more likely to smoke, and to smoke heavily, than their peers, because this brings about a lowering of the pitch of the voice even before medically assisted transition has begun. This means that they also face a higher than average risk of lung disease.

Both testosterone and smoking promote high blood pressure and high cholesterol, but in most cases this is easy to treat once it has been identified.

Although acne may sound like a trivial problem, it can be severe in some cases, and is particularly problematic for people who have pre-existing skin conditions. Patients may hesitate to report it because it seems minor to them in relation to the other issues they're dealing with, so it's important to be aware of it as a possibility if they show signs of skin irritation or pain.

Urethral stones can be a problem in later life for trans men who have had genital reconstruction. Although they are often very painful and can cause dangerous complications if ignored, in most cases they are easy to treat.

Trans women

On current evidence, trans women face an elevated risk of the following illnesses:

- high blood sugar

- blood clots

- high or low blood pressure

- silicone implant problems.

The major issues facing trans women can be traced to the use of oestrogen. Whereas oestrogen can lower blood pressure (sometimes leading to problems such as fainting, especially where blood sugar is also low), anti-androgens can raise it, so trans women can present with blood pressure that is too low *or* too high and extra caution should be taken if introducing additional medication to stabilise it.

Trans women are more likely than their peers to get breast implants and, in recent years, have increasingly opted for silicone implants in the hips and buttocks. As in other women, these sometimes prove problematic, especially where the treatment involved did not meet present-day UK standards. Because these treatments are rarely available on the NHS, some trans women travel abroad in search of them, and some are tempted by low-cost 'DIY' treatments. This makes them vulnerable to receiving low-quality implants which subsequently leak or migrate.

Interestingly, research to date suggests that trans women do not face an elevated risk of developing breast cancer – though, as in men, it remains a possibility.

Non-binary people

Non-binary people may not use any hormones or receive any surgery, or may use some of the elements associated with trans men or some associated with trans women, or a mixture of both. For this reason, their medical transition will usually need to be discussed in detail if they present with any of the health problems listed in this chapter.

Non-binary people face much the same elevated risks as other trans people in relation to substance abuse, addiction and injury, discussed below.

Overall concerns

It's important to remember that trans people often retain organs associated with their birth-assigned sex and can still face related health risks. These are magnified in situations where they are unable to access screening services.

Some trans people access medical services as little as possible because they feel unsafe about discussing their gender, especially if they are early in transition and have not yet come out to many people. This can mean that they don't get help with other health issues as early as they should.

Trans people who have not identified themselves as such to their doctors may still be taking hormones accessed on the black market. Even where these medications contain what they say they do, doses may be inconsistent, so it is important to discourage this practice, something most effectively done by providing access to prescribed hormones as quickly as possible.

Significant health problems can occur if trans people cease to take hormones abruptly. Any decrease in hormones taken (e.g. before planned surgery) should be carefully managed, and care should be taken to ensure that patients transferring between surgeries when moving house, or travelling abroad, will have access to an adequate supply. Where a patient has a mental health issue or learning disorder that means they are disorganised, extra support may be needed to ensure that they don't run out, especially over periods like Christmas when GPs are more difficult to access.

Trans people who have had their testes or ovaries removed but are not taking either oestrogen or testosterone face an elevated risk of developing osteoporosis. This is roughly the same as that found in postmenopausal women and the same approach should be taken to monitoring.

Intimate health issues

Trans people may be hesitant to talk about the kind of sex they are having because they have dysphoric feelings associated with it, because they worry that it will mean their gender is taken less seriously or simply because they expect a prejudiced response. This means that they are not always able to get the full benefit of sexual health services. It can be a barrier to diagnosis. When dealing with a trans patient in this situation, it helps to remind them that the discussion is confidential and that the more open they can be, the more easily you can ensure that they get the appropriate treatment if any is needed.

Trans men and non-binary people taking testosterone who have vaginally penetrative sex may suffer from injury because of thinning of the vaginal walls. The best treatment for this is a low-dose topical oestrogen cream, which will not normally have unwanted side effects.

The regular use of testosterone does not prevent the possibility of pregnancy. Those whose sexual habits mean they could get pregnant should discuss non-hormonal contraceptive options. It's possible for trans men and transmasculine non-binary people to have healthy pregnancies even after years on testosterone, but these should be properly planned and supported in order to ensure a healthy environment for the developing foetus.

Gay and bisexual trans men are sometimes turned away from screening and support services for men who have sex with men, because they are not perceived as 'real men'. There seems to be an assumption that if they are penetrated during sex, then it will be vaginal rather than anal, and they will not therefore face the same health risks. In fact, although some trans men enjoy being vaginally penetrated by male sex partners, many do not, and anal sex is a popular choice. This means that it's important to ensure that they can access the same services as gay and bisexual cis men.

A significant number of trans women, especially in urban areas, fund parts of their transition through sex work. This means that they face an increased risk of contracting sexually transmitted diseases and are also at increased risk of being on the receiving end of intimate partner violence, sexual assault and rape.

Trans women who retain their original genitals sometimes suffer injury as a result of tucking, a process which involves pushing the testicles inside the body and securing the penis between the legs. While this can be done relatively safely using surgical tape, inexperienced individuals may injure themselves by using other kinds of tape or by tucking for too long, especially if they're involved in physical activities that result in chafing. They should be advised to spend a few hours untucked every day and to keep their pubic hair short.

Tucking should be avoided by anyone who is trying to store sperm or conceive a child, as there is some evidence that it can lower the sperm count.

Substance abuse and addiction

Trans people are more likely than their peers to take recreational drugs including alcohol and controlled substances, probably as a consequence of the experience of prejudice[49] and, all too often, familial rejection. In addition to this, trans men may drink heavily as a means of asserting their masculinity. This means that they face an increased risk of developing addictions.

Support services for people facing addiction issues are often based around religious ideas and may not be accepting of trans people. It's important to ensure that any such organisation will respect the gender of the patient before making a referral.

Trans people may face additional difficulties in overcoming addiction because of the social element involved. It can be harder for them to break away from friends or family members who have the same habit, simply because they find it harder to forge new social connections or are too intimidated by the prospect to try. Remaining in close social contact with other addicts and maintaining the same social habits is associated with an increased risk of relapse.

Trans men who smoke may be hesitant about trying to give up because damage to the throat caused by smoking can make them sound more masculine. Attempts to persuade them to quit can be more effective if accompanied by advice on voice masculinisation techniques. The New York Speech and Voice Lab[50] has some good free advice available online.

Injury

Trans people are significantly more likely than members of the general population to seek medical care as a result of injury, although support organisations believe that transphobic hate crime is significantly under-reported and that many of its victims don't seek treatment even when they probably should. Rates of assault against trans people are significantly elevated, with one survey finding that 35% of those between the ages of 16 and 25 reported having experienced physical assault motivated by transphobic prejudice on at least one occasion.[51] This is especially worrying for disabled people, not only because they are generally less able to defend themselves (and, in some cases, much more likely to suffer serious harm), but because having a disability already places an individual at greater risk of assault.[52]

Facial injury can be particularly distressing for trans women and some non-binary people because it compromises their ability to present a feminine appearance in accordance with standard social expectations. Healthcare staff providing assistance need to be sensitive to this.

Disclosure

Regardless of the medical issue under discussion, healthcare providers should be aware that trans people may conceal some of their symptoms for one or more of the following reasons:

- associated dysphoria that makes discussing the subject distressing

- fear of being denied medical support with transition

- fear of having established hormone treatment discontinued.

Most trans people do care about their general health and will disclose symptoms that seem to them to suggest something serious, but they may conceal those they believe they can endure or manage by themselves, such as chronic pain, cramping, syncope (fainting caused by insufficient blood flow to the brain) or depression. This can present a barrier to the accurate diagnosis of a wide range of health problems.

Where individuals hesitate to disclose chronic health problems to a doctor, they may be more willing to do so with a trusted nurse – for instance, at a well person clinic. If asked to promise not to tell the doctor, such a person can then discuss the matter with a doctor on a hypothetical basis and let the patient know if the problem could indicate something serious. This intermediary approach reduces the long-term risk of serious problems going undetected.

7

Sensory Impairments and Disability

People with sensory impairments do not necessarily consider themselves to be disabled. Where care provision is concerned, however, many of the same issues come into play. Furthermore, trans people with sensory impairments often experience the effects of intersectional prejudice in similar ways, especially when it comes to social isolation or the denial of their identities. Being alert to these issues can help health and social care providers to support them more effectively and improve their access to key services.

Deaf and hearing-impaired people

The experience of being Deaf or hearing-impaired affects trans people in three significant ways. First, it can present them with social difficulties over and above those associated with each characteristic on its own. Second, it can restrict their access to resources, information and support. Third, it can make it difficult to change the vocal cues that non-impaired people use to determine gender.

Social factors

Like all minority communities, the Deaf community can provide a strong sense of social support and a distinct cultural identity.

This is extremely important to most of its members. It's important for outsiders to understand that this goes beyond what is conferred by support groups for most disabilities and illnesses because Deaf people are bound together by shared experiences of perception and language, factors that have a profound effect on the way one understands and thinks about the world.

The flip side of being in such a community is that it increases the risks associated with social rejection. Although there are many openly trans and Deaf people out there, and although much of the Deaf community is supportive of trans rights, this may not be the case with every local community. Trans people may feel that there is nobody around like themselves, may struggle to find role models or may worry that they will be outright rejected by their community, making it very difficult for them to find a supportive social environment.

Deaf people who routinely communicate in sign language usually learn their signing from their local community, as there is relatively little media content that includes signing (and the majority of what is available is in American Sign Language (ASL) rather than British Sign Language (BSL) – there are significant differences). This means that they may lack the signs to talk about being transgender or, for instance, to say that they are non-binary, even if they are familiar with the written terms. Finger spelling can be used to work around this problem, but it's comparatively slow and not well suited to situations like coming out, which can be highly emotive and prone to misunderstanding.

It should not be assumed that Deaf people will change the signs they use for their personal names when they transition, even if they change their written or spoken names. Signed names don't always relate closely to names in English and although some convey gender, not all do.

Access to resources

For young people growing up and exploring gender issues today, vlogs – video channels hosted by individuals – are a very important means of finding role models and community. They're a source of information about everything from hormones and surgery to binding and make-up techniques. They are, however, very rarely subtitled. This means that people with hearing impairments can be cut off from an important source of support. Although there are an increasing number of pieces of software available for translating speech into written words, they're not very sophisticated and work only for a narrow range of accents. The frequency with which they make errors means that it would be unwise to rely on them for anything that might have health or safety implications.

Because sign language interpreters are in short supply, Deaf and hearing-impaired people can also struggle with things such as talking to their doctors. It's one thing to manage when explaining about something like an injured knee, but quite another to try to take the first steps in obtaining access to treatment for gender dysphoria. As interpreters are likely to be needed at every stage of the transition journey, often in different parts of the country where there are no personal connections to help speed things up, Deaf and hearing-impaired people can face further delays in what is already a slow process.

If you run a health or social care service or informational resource where you normally communicate by telephone, offering the option of text message communication can make it much more accessible for Deaf and hearing-impaired people. Texting or typing into a laptop can also be the best option for communication in consultations where no interpreter is available. Even if it's only used as back-up, it significantly reduces the risk of miscommunication. Information about how to take medication, such as hormones, should always be provided in written form.

Vocal issues

For people with profound hearing impairment, it can be almost impossible to change the vocal cues commonly used to signal gender. People who have never been able to hear may struggle to imagine what the world is like for people who have access to these cues instantly, and consequently find it difficult to cope with persistently being identified as trans by strangers even if, visually, they don't look at all obvious.

People in this position are generally familiar with the idea of high and low, loud and quiet noises, because they experience them as vibrations. Placing two fingers against the Adam's apple is the easiest way to tell by touch what the pitch of an individual's voice is. By practising this on themselves, it's possible for Deaf and hearing-impaired people to adjust their voices, but as they also face the same challenges as other trans people in doing this, it requires a lot of effort. Even if they rarely try to communicate vocally, even small exclamations in an untutored voice can quickly give away transness and potentially expose an individual to transphobia or simply force them to be out when they don't want to be – so it's a significant issue.

Blind and visually impaired people

Trans people who are blind or visually impaired face social difficulties, difficulties in accessing information and difficulties with presentation.

Social factors

To get an idea of the kind of social difficulties that trans people with visual impairments have to deal with, consider this: almost everyone in this intersectional group has been asked, at least once, how they can know that they're trans when they can't see what people of different genders look like.[53] Some report that they've been asked it on a frequent basis. Think about it for a moment. If you close your eyes, do you cease to be aware of what your own body is like? Do you get no clues about gender from the way people feel, smell or sound? It's obvious that gender remains part of life, yet this is just one example of the ways in which bind trans people have their identities challenged.

Many blind people find it difficult to maintain an active social life because they have difficulty getting around independently and also have to deal with prejudice related to their impairment. The idea of putting fragile social networks in jeopardy by coming out as trans can be extremely intimidating. Meanwhile, trans support groups and social groups are not always very accessible for blind people, and there's no guarantee that they will be welcoming.

People who have guide dogs to help them often report that their dogs start behaving differently towards them when they first start taking hormones. Dogs smell the difference in body chemistry long before the development of physical changes that are apparent to humans. Taking oestrogen doesn't seem to lead to any problems, but taking testosterone may result in male dogs – even after neutering – becoming very excitable. Although they adjust over time, extra help may be needed in the meantime to ensure that they remember their training and are able to do their jobs properly.

Access to information

Historically, blind and visually impaired people have faced significant barriers in access to information, but easy access to screen readers means that this is now far less of a problem, with more and more material available online. It remains important, however, to have online versions of information leaflets and to avoid the use of PDFs (unless alternative formats are also available) because they can't always be read by screen readers. Web pages should be designed with screen readers in mind and text descriptions of images, tables, charts and diagrams should be provided.

Many blind people use recording devices so they can revisit information imparted during consultations and keep track of it properly. It's important for service providers to allow this even in contexts where they are normally very careful to limit the risk of discussions being leaked, as can be the case with transition support services.

Presentation

Most blind people have the same sense of what they want to look like and how they want to present themselves as anyone else. Adjusting that personal style to suit a changing body and send a different message about gender can, however, be a challenge for anybody and visual impairment adds an extra layer of complication. Hairstyles, clothes and shoes (which also need to be safe to walk in when inevitably tripping and stumbling more than most people) all need to be reconsidered. Trans women may need help with make-up, if they choose to wear it, and with masking any residual facial hair until it can be removed. Trans men may need help with new facial hair. In both cases, people with long-standing severe visual impairments may need help understanding the social cues that different kinds of presentation can send. They may want to try to look older or younger, professional or casual, show affiliation with a particular subculture, look flirtatious or present themselves in accordance with their religious or cultural affiliations.

People who have a limited field of vision may know exactly how they want to present themselves but still need help with aspects of personal grooming in order to get the desired effect.

Deafblind people

Living with both auditory and visual impairments presents unique challenges. Deafblind people are especially likely to suffer from social isolation, meaning that coming out as trans is an enormous social risk. Especially where they have become deafblind in later life, there is a risk that they will be unable to communicate with anyone except their carers, making them particularly vulnerable to abuse and neglect – a problem that becomes still more acute if they are also at risk of encountering transphobic prejudice.

Most deafblind people have some degree of sight or hearing but they may still need support to manage day-to-day tasks, especially in places where there is a lot of ambient noise or visual intrusion (shopping malls, where there are a lot of people moving about and a lot of advertising designed to catch the eye, can be particularly difficult to navigate). These issues can make it difficult to manage group communication, making trans or LGBT (lesbian, gay, bisexual and transgender) support groups inaccessible. If you are supporting somebody in this situation, you can help by attending a support group with them or on their behalf and asking if anybody there is willing to meet with them one on one. Bear in mind that trans people will often be wary about meeting a stranger alone in a non-busy place; nevertheless, it's often possible to find solutions that work all round, such as meeting in a quiet room of an LGBT centre or meeting in the presence of friends who agree to keep their own talking and movement to a minimum.

Braille

Where means of communication are limited, so is access to information. Many blind and deafblind people read Braille, but it's rare for materials aimed at minority populations to be available in Braille format.

Some leaflets about trans healthcare and support services can be ordered from the government in Braille format, but these focus on providing assistance with practical planning. What most trans people feel a need for, especially in the early stags of thinking about their relationship with gender, is information aimed at helping them to explore gender issues and information about the emotional experiences of other people who have gone through transition.

8

Mental Health Issues and Transgender People

In 2011, the World Professional Association for Transgender Health (WPATH) formally recognised that being transgender is not in itself a disorder and that attempting to 'cure' it with reparative therapy is both impractical and unethical. From that point onwards, discussion around supporting trans people's mental health has focused on dealing with issues *associated* with being trans, which may stem from the experience of gender dysphoria or the experience of prejudice and discrimination. These problems are more common in trans people than in the general population, but that doesn't mean they are directly caused by being trans. There is evidence, however, that some of these issues decline significantly after hormonal or surgical transition.

Anxiety

Any situation in which people struggle to fit in socially increases the risk of developing anxiety. For trans people, this often begins in childhood, when many first begin to realise that they don't fit society's expectations. One recent study found that rates of probable anxiety disorders are three times higher among trans people than in the general population,[54] and that trans men are more likely to suffer from them than trans women, with the risk for women dropping once they started hormone treatment.

Social anxiety is a particular problem for many trans people because of the fear of encountering hostility. This may mean not wanting to leave the house at all except when it's unavoidable, or it may mean being intimidated by new situations, such as the prospect of joining a new hobby group or visiting a new dentist. It tends to be more acute in situations where gender is a significant social concern, such as when using public toilets or being part of a group divided into men and women for a workplace training activity.

For disabled people, anxiety disorders can be compounded by the frequent need for hypervigilance and detailed planning in order to ensure that it's possible to get around successfully and stay safe through the course of the day. It can also be harder for disabled people to eat healthily and engage in regular exercise, two factors known to be associated with decreased anxiety levels.

Depression

From an early age, many trans people have very low expectations of life. They may frequently encounter prejudice, they may be afraid to express who they really are and they may perceive themselves as having few prospects in life. All these factors can contribute to the development of depression.

Trans people who suffer from depression sometimes find it harder to transition. They may feel that things will never get better for them no matter what they do, and they may fear that the social and emotional challenges of transition will be too much for them to cope with. There is, however, some evidence that taking cross-sex hormones leads to a direct reduction in depression in trans men. It has been noted that serotonin reuptake transporter (SERT) bonding, which is reduced in people suffering from major depression, increases in trans men when they take testosterone, although it decreases in trans women when they take oestrogen.[55] Another study notes that both perceived stress levels and measurable cortisol levels are lower in trans people receiving cross-hormone treatment.[56]

Post-traumatic stress disorder (PTSD)

Trans people are more likely than members of the wider population to have experienced family breakdown or mental, physical or sexual abuse. They face an elevated risk of domestic abuse, as do people with physical disabilities.[57] Furthermore, physical disability and serious illness can themselves be associated with traumatic events. All of this means that disabled and chronically ill trans people are more likely than most people to suffer from PTSD. Furthermore, PTSD can result from cumulative negative experiences even in the absence of specific major trauma events, with one recent study showing a connection between PTSD symptoms and everyday discrimination.[58]

Self-harm

A 2017 survey by Stonewall Scotland found that 96% of young trans people in Scotland have deliberately harmed themselves at one point or another, comparing this with an NHS estimate that around 10% of young people in the UK general population have done so.[59] Self-harm may be related to underlying anxiety or depression. Over time, scars resulting from self-harm can themselves become a cause of stress. Although it does not usually involve suicidal intent, some forms of self-harm, such as cutting with blades, carry a significant risk of accidental injury. It has also been argued that getting used to self-harming behaviour means that if suicidal ideation later develops, there is less of an instinctive barrier to prevent a person from acting on it.[60]

Self-harm scars can be a source of social discomfort for people who cannot conceal them from nurses or care workers because of the type of assistance they need. If the scars are clearly old – like others, trans people are most likely to self-harm during their teens and 20s – then it is usually best just to ignore them. If the patient or client is clearly upset about them being noticed at all, it can be worth noting in a calm way that you see a lot of people with scars. This provides reassurance that you don't think they should be a source of shame and leaves open the option of talking about them so that somebody who is still struggling with related feelings can ask for help.

If you see fresh scars on a patient or client that you believe could be a result of self-harm, you should be aware that they could be an indicator of acute stress. Expressing shock or strong concern can add to this stress and can also cause feelings of guilt or shame. A better option is to find out if they have access to counselling or psychiatric services and, if they don't, calmly let them know that such services are available and advise on how they can be accessed.

Suicidal ideation

The Stonewall Scotland survey referenced above found that 98% of young trans people in Scotland have thought about suicide, and noted that research by Young Minds suggests the rate for the general population is around 25%. Stonewall Scotland found that 45% of young trans people in Scotland have actually attempted suicide at least once. A 2012 survey of trans people in Ireland[61] found that 78% had thought about suicide (63% of them within the past year) and 40% had attempted suicide at least once. Significantly, 81% said that their suicidal ideation was more severe before they transitioned.

In light of these observations, it's vital that expressions of suicidal ideation by trans people are taken seriously. Furthermore, disabled people have been found to be four times more likely than their non-disabled peers to have attempted suicide (after adjusting for other major contributory factors such as socioeconomic status),[62] and there is evidence that the number of suicide attempts among disabled people in the UK has increased significantly in recent years.[63] With the exception of chronic pain, which is a major contributory factor, research suggests that this is less likely to be associated with physical limitations or difficulties than with financial concerns or difficulties in keeping up with day-to-day household tasks. This suggests that carers can play a significant role in reducing the risk of suicide both by helping their clients to manage at home and by providing reassurance – for example, advising clients with chronic fatigue that it's understandable if they can't manage everything and no reasonable person would think they were just being lazy.

Eating disorders

Studies have shown that trans people are significantly more likely to suffer from eating disorders than their cis peers.[64] There are several theories as to why this could be. It has been postulated that anorexia in adolescence sometimes occurs as a reaction to unwanted bodily changes and an attempt to regain control over the body.[65] It has also been suggested that eating disorders are about an attempt to conform to social pressures to be thin in order to meet social standards of what the ideal man or woman is supposed to look like – pressures that can affect trans people more strongly than their cis peers because they may already feel inadequate in regard to their gender presentation. It is also thought that eating disorders can be a maladaptive coping response to transphobic prejudice and discrimination. Eating disorders bear some similarities to addictions,[66] which trans people are generally more vulnerable to.

Traditionally, dealing with this type of comorbidity has led to gender dysphoria being treated as a less significant issue that can wait until the eating disorder has been stabilised before it is dealt with. Growing awareness of the mental health risks of untreated dysphoria are, however, beginning to change this thinking, especially as it's more difficult to stabilise an eating disorder in a patient who is suffering from ongoing stress. A Finnish study undertaken in 2012[67] observed that undergoing physical transition seems to alleviate the symptoms of eating disorders and improve individuals' ability to develop healthy eating habits.

Because most eating disorders are never fully cured but leave the sufferer continually vulnerable to lapsing into unhealthy behaviour, care providers should be wary if they discover that a trans patient or client seems to be exhibiting symptoms, and should check whether or not they have a history of such problems. This is especially the case at times of stress, when additional support may be needed to avoid a serious relapse. It is important to note, however, that eating disorders are often associated with a desire to be in control,[68] so you must be careful not to make the person you are caring for feel disempowered, which could make the situation worse.

General mental health issues

Trans people also experience mental health issues that have nothing to do with them being trans, at the same rates as members of the general population. These can present them with specific problems. Some report that they find it difficult to access treatment because of the assumption that, being trans, they need to be treated by people with expertise in trans-related care. People who do have that expertise may lack sufficient expertise to treat their other problems, so that trans people find themselves shuttled between departments with no one actually giving them the help they need. It's really important for service providers to understand that in circumstances like these it doesn't matter if they are new to trans issues as long as they are respectful and patients are comfortable with the situation – being trans is not a factor in every mental health problem affecting a trans person.

Where a trans person develops a serious mental health problem before coming out, it can complicate their attempts to demonstrate to medical professionals that they are trans and make it harder for them to access treatment. It's understandable that there may be concerns when, for instance, an individual with a history of delusional disorders claims to be trans, and yet such people are still just as likely to be genuinely trans as anybody else. Situations like this need to be handled with sensitivity. It should not be assumed that it's impossible that the individual is genuinely trans.

Intersectional prejudice

People with mental health problems are often the targets of prejudice. Where this is compounded by transphobia, specific problems can emerge.

Trans women who have difficulty controlling their emotions or coping with social situations are often perceived as sexually aggressive.

Trans men who suffer from depression or anxiety are often told that this is a result of internalised homophobia, that they are unable to come to terms with being lesbians and that this is the cause of their desire to transition. (Even trans men who have only ever been attracted to men report encountering this kind of prejudice.)

Trans people who are neurodivergent or have difficulty expressing themselves are often treated as victims and considered incapable of knowing their own gender. They are sometimes told that their gender has been imposed on them by other people because they couldn't possibly have chosen it for themselves. Carers can also be targets where this kind of prejudice emerges.

Minority stress

Many mental healthcare practitioners consider minority stress to be a significant factor in contributing to poor mental health among trans people. According to the prevailing thinking on this subject, being a member of a minority group means that an individual is subject to additional stress factors over time, and that these have a cumulative effect. Experience of prejudice and discrimination, socioeconomic disadvantage and lack of social support can all factor into this. This then leads to the development of internal proximal stressors – for instance, thinking a lot about past encounters with hostile individuals or internalising stigma – resulting in ongoing psychological damage and potentially leading to poor mental and physical health outcomes.

Trans experiences of good mental health

Despite all this, there are many trans people who don't have diagnoses of mental illness, and some who report that they have happy, fulfilling lives. What seems to be universal about the latter is that they have good social support networks. Most have not experienced family rejection, or have moved beyond it to re-establish positive family relationships. Good friends and friendly, accepting neighbours also seem to be a significant stabilising influence.

The fact that being trans is not inevitably linked with mental illness is one of the reasons it ceased to be classified as a mental illness itself. There is now a major research focus on better understanding the nature and psychological effects of transphobia, with the aim of giving trans people the tools to build resilience and better protect their mental health, even in hostile environments.

9

Sex-Specific Service Provision

The provision of some medical services is separated by sex for very practical reasons. Some ailments are found almost exclusively in men or almost exclusively in women. This is complicated when it comes to trans people, which is why it's important for GPs to know if a patient has a trans history. That patient may still need access to routine scans available to people of their birth-assigned gender, and may need hospital treatment in facilities entirely geared towards that gender.

In addition to this, services for victims of violence may be sex-segregated in order to reduce stress for those using them. Historically, this has meant that trans victims had nowhere to go. Today, new strategies are being used to ensure that trans people can receive support and to allay any related fears among cis service users.

Smear tests

Although some trans men have total hysterectomies as part of the process of transition, many do not. If the cervix remains, they continue to face a risk of developing cervical cancer. Contrary to what some doctors assume, many trans men routinely play a receptive role in vaginal penetrative sex, so it should not be assumed that their risk is decreased because of a change in sexual habits. This means that in most cases they should still receive regular pap smears if they are over the age of 25.

Undergoing a smear test is upsetting for many patients and can be particularly difficult for trans men, who may find that it aggravates their dysphoria. It's particularly important that they do not feel their gender identity is compromised or disrespected during the process. Where letters are mailed out automatically to patients who are due for smear tests, it's important that those going to trans men are flagged up so as to avoid the use of incorrect titles and pronouns. It is equally important to ensure that trans men are not accidentally removed from lists by untrained staff members who think their names must be there by mistake. If such a letter is sent to a cis man by accident, he will probably just laugh it off. If it is *not* sent to a trans man who needs it, the consequences could be fatal.

Although some trans men are unhappy about being asked to have smear tests, it is clearly in the interests of their health that they do so, so asking should be the default, while reminding them that they can opt out if they wish to.

Some non-binary people also experience dysphoria when having smear tests done. They are at a higher risk of being misgendered if they look less masculine, so it's important for staff to pay attention and make sure they're using appropriate language.

Cancer Research recently replaced the word 'women' with the term 'everyone with a cervix' in the materials it uses to promote smear tests out of concern that trans men and non-binary people were not accessing tests at the rate they should.

HPV vaccination

Several strains of this common sexually transmitted disease are known to increase the risk of cervical cancer, and two strains have been found to be involved in 70% of all cervical cancer cases.[69] The human papillomavirus (HPV) vaccine is understood to be effective in persons of either sex, yet in the UK it was initially offered to girls only because the associated cancer risks are higher in girls. NHS Scotland[70] and NHS Wales[71] made their vaccination programmes gender-neutral in July 2018.

Earlier in 2018, NHS England announced its intention to vaccinate trans boys – because they share the same risks as cis girls – *and* to vaccinate trans girls, for two reasons. First, because doing so means that they will not be marked out and separated from their peers; second, because trans girls are statistically more likely than cis boys to end up engaged in sex work or other risky sexual behaviours, and are therefore at higher risk of exposure to HPV.

This change of policy was mischaracterised in the press,[72] but it's important to note that there are sound medical reasons behind it. It has now been superseded by a decision to extend vaccination to all boys in England.[73]

At the time of writing, Northern Ireland continues to have a vaccination programme that is open only to cis girls. Individual clinics and GP surgeries can decide whether or not to provide it to trans children, and should consider the issues mentioned here.

Mammograms

Even if they have had their breasts removed, trans men remain at higher risk of breast cancer than most of the male population. There are two reasons for this. First, if they are not closely monitored, they may have too much testosterone in their blood; testosterone that is not picked up by receptors is converted into oestrogen, which can trigger breast cancer just as it does in women. Second, if they feel uncomfortable about their breasts or chest area, they are less likely to conduct regular self-examinations, so they are slow to spot signs of tumours developing and less likely to get them removed before they become problematic. On account of this, it is important that trans men over the age of 50 receive regular mammograms. NHS England recommends that they be carried out every three years. Trans men who are registered as male with their GPs will not automatically be contacted about this and will need a GP referral in order to get a mammogram carried out.

People who find it difficult to stand and keep still for five minutes should inform the mammography unit of this before attending, as there may or may not be suitable facilities for providing them with this service. If it's not possible, they will often be able to be referred to another unit which is able to help.

Prostate cancer screening

There is no national prostate cancer screening programme on the NHS because the test isn't 100% reliable and further exploration would not be medically justified in most cases, but it is important for cis men and trans women who have a family history of prostate cancer, are of black ethnic origin or are overweight. It can be carried out by a GP, but many do not realise that prostate cancer remains a risk for trans women.

Abdominal aortic aneurysm screening

It is recommended that trans women consider getting an abdominal aortic aneurysm screening at the age of 65, as cis men do, even though they will not automatically be called for it if they are registered as female with their GPs. Because testosterone is known to be a major contributor to poor cardiovascular health, this is particularly important for trans women who have transitioned late in life or who have not had their testes removed and don't take anti-androgens. Trans women can arrange referral through their GPs if necessary and can contact the screening department in advance if they have any concerns about their privacy.

Trans men should also ensure that they are screened, arranging referrals if they are still registered as female with their GPs. This is particularly important for trans men who have transitioned early in life, with later transitioners and trans men who don't take testosterone at lower risk.

'Men's diseases' and 'women's diseases'

Trans people often report that they suffer from additional difficulties if they have illnesses strongly associated with one sex or another, such as haemophilia or Becker muscular dystrophy. Specialists in these areas tend to work only with patients of one sex and may find it more than usually difficult to adjust to patients who don't fit this expectation. This may lead to trans patients feeling that their gender is not respected or is treated as an affectation, because as well as failing to fit social gender-related expectations they fail to fit the disease model.

Clinics dealing with diseases like this may not have facilities such as private changing rooms. In this situation, special arrangements need to be made so that trans patients can access the full range of services and do so with dignity.

Support for survivors of sexual violence and domestic abuse

When rape crisis centres and refuges for those fleeing domestic violence first began to appear, they were strictly for women only. Over the past two decades, such services have become available for men. They are frequently segregated by sex, however, which can make it difficult for trans people to get help. Some trans victims of rape and sexual assault report being turned away by both women's and men's services.

In this area, Scotland and Wales are taking the lead. Rape Crisis Scotland has offered a trans-inclusive service for several years (retaining the right to exclude any person, trans or cis, whose behaviour suggests that they are a risk to others). Fearless is a Scottish service that specialises in supporting men, including trans men, and extends its services to non-binary people. Welsh Women's Aid is also committed to trans inclusion. In England, policies on inclusion vary between different local services, but outright rejection is now rare. Support for victims of sexual violence in Northern Ireland is thin on the ground but broadly trans-inclusive.

Based in Brighton, the Trans Survivors Switchboard offers telephone support to trans people of all kinds from all across the UK. It can also help to put people in touch with other forms of support in some cases, and help trans people to identify the nearest crisis centre where they can be confident of receiving support. Cyfannol offers a similar service to domestic abuse victims seeking help in Wales.

Trans people experiencing domestic abuse can face additional difficulties. They may have their hormones withheld by their partners or face threats to tell people they have not come out to that they are trans, if they do not do what their partner demands. They are often bullied in relation to the fact that they're trans, reinforcing low self-worth. Abusers often convince their victims to stay by telling them that no one else would want them, and that's easier to do with people who have experienced social exclusions or expressions of disgust at their appearance because they are trans. Disabled people are in a similar position – they may have care that they need withheld so that they go hungry or are forced to sit in their own faeces; they believe that nobody will want them because they are disabled. People who are both trans and disabled are very vulnerable to this kind of controlling behaviour.

Trans men can have difficulty acknowledging that they are victims of domestic abuse or sexual violence because, like cis men, they fear that it will undermine their masculinity, but unlike most cis men they have often had to struggle really hard to have their masculinity acknowledged at all. They may also find that they can't talk about the details of what happened to them without outing themselves, or that in order to do so they have to discuss aspects of their bodies that they found distressing to think about even before they were assaulted.

Research by Stonewall found that service providers in this sector use a variety of techniques to ensure that other service users are comfortable with the presence of trans people. These range from talking about the emotional experiences that all those seeking help there share to bringing in religious speakers to talk about the importance of inclusion.[74]

In a survey by the Scottish Transgender Alliance,[75] 80% of respondents reported having experienced some form of emotional, sexual or physically abusive behaviour by a partner or ex-partner; for 47%, sexual abuse was involved.

GP diagnoses

Most GPs are used to thinking of a patient's sex as one of the primary factors when making a first-stage diagnosis based on symptoms shown or reported to them. For instance, when a woman presents with symptoms of anaemia, they are likely to think first of low iron levels and put the possibility of sickle cell anaemia a long way down the list, whereas that balance of probability shifts when the patient is a man. With trans people (as with intersex people) this is more complicated – an individual patient could fall into either the male risk group or the female risk group depending on the disease. It's important for GPs to try to overcome their habitual approach in this situation.

10

Data Management

Trans people can be placed at risk if their data is leaked, and trans people who are seriously ill or disabled are doubly vulnerable, so it is particularly important to be careful about how data is managed. In many cases details revealing that a person is trans are considered to be sensitive information under the terms of the Data Protection Act,[76] and further obligations can apply where an individual has a gender recognition certificate (issued in accordance with the terms of the Gender Recognition Act[77]).

The Data Protection Act and GDPR

The Data Protection Act (2018), incorporating the General Data Protection Regulation (GDPR) from EU law, gives health and care professionals a special duty of confidentiality when it comes to dealing with personal data. It sets out six basic principles that must be adhered to, requiring that personal data should be:

- processed in a legal and fair way
- processed for specific, explicit and legitimate reasons
- adequate, relevant and not excessive
- accurate and up to date
- kept for no longer than necessary
- processed and maintained securely.

The act further requires that data should not be processed or archived in a way that is likely to cause serious damage or distress to the person it concerns.

The GDPR gives individuals the right to access their records and rectify mistakes.

If you have concerns about your specific obligations under the Data Protection Act and GDPR, the Information Commissioner's Office can advise. There are also a number of fact sheets on their website that you may find helpful.[78]

What NHS guidelines say

In 2012, the NHS issued guidelines advising GP practices in England and Wales to retain relevant clinical information on transitioning patients but remove 'all references to the previous name, gender and NHS number', along with anything from which that information might be derived. The idea is that a patient's past gender should be disregarded except in specific contexts where it might factor into future health needs. Nobody who glances casually at a patient's notes, rather than looking for something specific within them, should be able to see that the patient has transitioned.

In Scotland, both the NHS number and the CHI number (a Community Health Index number that is unique to each patient registered with NHS Scotland) will normally need to be changed. When a patient's gender is changed in the computer system, practitioner services will contact the patient to check that they're happy about the changes being made.

It is possible that a trans person could demand that every reference to their previously recorded gender and transition be removed from their notes, or that their notes be erased. While there would be some legal grounds for that, it's obviously something that could potentially place that individual at risk. In such a case, a doctor should work through the records with the individual to discuss any areas of concern. Some trans people report that their GP surgeries have taken this approach without any demands being made, helping to safeguard their right to privacy without, in the process, losing information that could be needed to ensure appropriate treatment for medical problems arising in the future.

In order to be compliant with the Equality Act (2010), you must ensure that it is no more difficult for a trans person to get their details altered than it is for anybody else. For instance, a change of name should be as straightforward for a trans person as it is for a woman who has decided to adopt her husband's name after getting married.

Trans people dread being in situations where receptionists call out their names with the wrong title attached, outing them in front of everybody in the waiting room – something that happens all too often and is frequently a result of poor data management, as evidenced by a recent case in Teesside.[79] They can also occur as a result of another commonplace but deeply problematic action – doctors issuing prescription using their old names or titles, which leads to them being outed when they go to collect their medicine; they cannot be sure that pharmacy staff will be accepting or that they will be sufficiently well trained not to out them to other members of the public who are in the pharmacy when they call out to say that a prescription is ready. This may seem like a matter of offence or embarrassment, but what trans people fear – with some justification – is that it will lead to them being assaulted.

Despite the availability of the NHS guidance, trans people report that they are often told their NHS numbers cannot be changed, or even that it's not possible to change their names and titles.

In 2014 it emerged that the Medical Defence Union (MDU) was answering GP queries to the effect that patients' pre-transition records should continue to reflect their gender as it was recognised at the time. This potentially conflicts with the requirements of the Data Protection Act. It seems to have been removed from the

MDU's website since, but may account for some of the confusion around this issue.

Screening call-outs

When organising changes to personal data records, you should discuss the issue of screening programmes with the patient. Many of these are sex-specific. Most trans people feel that attending them, and thus reducing the risk of developing certain diseases, is more important than avoiding the potential dysphoria triggered by call-outs or the procedures themselves, but this is not the case for everyone.

Once an agreement is made about how to proceed in relation to screenings, it should be signed by both parties and dated. If the patient decides not to receive call-outs, this can be recorded as a decision to opt out without a specific reason needing to be given; it is therefore not necessary to reference transition in somebody's notes in order to remove screening notices which could give away that person's trans status from their notes. Patients who opt out should be advised that they are free to reverse that decision at any point if they change their minds.

See Chapter 9 on sex-specific service provision for further information on trans people and screening programmes.

Collecting data

Managing patient or client data effectively is only possible if you can be confident that you are getting the right data in the first place. This means that trans people need to feel safe sharing their information. They need to be confident that they won't encounter prejudice or discrimination from you or your staff, and they need to be confident that information that could make them vulnerable will be securely stored.

When collecting data, it's important not to make assumptions. Trans patients frequently report seeing medical personnel filling out forms with their data in front of them, asking about some details but not bothering to ask about others, and filling in the wrong gender details or even names that they no longer use.

Non-binary people may be particularly hesitant to be open about their gender with care providers, for several reasons. First, if they are not seeking medical help to transition (some do, but this is less common than in the binary trans population), they do not have an incentive to come out for that reason. They are less likely to present themselves in ways that are clearly at odds with societal expectations of their assigned gender, especially if they were assigned female (a person believed to be male in a skirt turns heads; a person believed to be female in trousers does not), so they are less likely to feel that they will be identified anyway and would therefore do better to be open about it. They may also believe that it would be pointless due to an assumption that there will be no system in which their correct gender, pronoun choices, title, etc. can be recorded.

Keeping records of the above-mentioned details and ensuring that staff treat non-binary people with respect, and making it clear to all patients that this is your policy (for instance, by mentioning it on your website and on posters in your waiting room), means they are more likely to be open with you. This can enhance their general confidence and feelings of trust towards your staff. It also makes it easier for you to identify specific health needs they may have in relation to their gender.

Software issues

One frequently reported problem with recording trans people's data appropriately stems from the difficulty of getting software to cooperate. IT service providers may need to be contacted to resolve this and to deal with any instances of systems resetting themselves so that old data reappears after a database has been refreshed.

Where it is not possible to record a non-binary patient's gender in the computer system, this should be discussed with them. A prominent note should be made to reduce the risk of misgendering. In some systems it is possible to record a gender-neutral title such as Mx or Per. If the patient considers this appropriate, it can be a helpful way of signalling their gender.

Within the practice

Under section 22 of the Gender Recognition Act, it is an offence to disclose the trans status of any person who has a gender recognition certificate. This means that an individual's trans status should not be discussed even within the practice unless explicit permission has been given for this. A trans person who has just come out to a doctor or a practice nurse, for instance, may not feel comfortable with anyone else knowing. Where somebody is going through transition, however, it is difficult to avoid other staff knowing. In this case the matter should be discussed with the patient, who should be advised of which staff will need to know and reassured that the information will not go any further. In most cases, patients are happy for all staff to know provided that they can be assured that the matter will otherwise be kept confidential and that they will be treated with respect.

Making referrals

When making a referral to a specialist, you should disclose the minimum amount of information necessary for them to do their job. For instance, if you are referring a patient for an eye examination, there is no need to disclose that they are trans at all. If you are referring a patient to a urologist, you will need to reference any genital surgery they have had, but there is not normally any need to comment on other aspects of their transition, such as top surgery.

Trans patients who are being referred to specialists should be told how much has been disclosed and advised that they may need to disclose more themselves if gender-related issues emerge in the course of treatment. For instance, a trans man who has had facial implants will need to disclose them if he is referred for an MRI scan.

Consistency of data

Trans people generally try really hard to change their personal data in the same way with every organisation that holds it, but problems can still arise. Sometimes an organisation is overlooked. Sometimes requests to change data are met with refusal to cooperate. Sometimes data is changed and then reverts when a database is restored from back-up, or a staff member notices that it has been changed, assumes an error must have been made and changes it back. This is particularly problematic for non-binary people who use non-standard titles. They may also find that different organisations are able to change different parts (but not necessarily all) of their data, depending on the software in use. In some cases, binary trans people find that they are able to get every other bit of their data changed except their actual gender designation, because some organisations will not do this unless and until a gender recognition certificate has been issued.

As a result, trans people's records may not always match. It's important not to leap to the assumption that something fraudulent is going on. Computer systems may flag up differences as suspicious and a bit of human intelligence is then needed to sort things out.

Consistency issues can be problematic in communication between doctors and care agencies or between doctors and the Department for Work and Pensions (DWP) staff, even when all concerned are trying to do their best for the person whose data is involved. This is an issue that is likely to become less prominent as more and more systems are designed with trans people in mind, as policies become more inclusive and software is updated, but at present it can be difficult to deal with. It's important that trans people are not blamed for this – unless they are senior IT designers whose products are used by the organisations concerned, bureaucratic inconsistencies are not their fault.

11

Inpatient Hospital Care

Trans people going into hospital are often concerned that they will be treated in ways inappropriate to their gender, or even that they may encounter prejudice. Sadly, some trans people do have negative experiences like this. This can happen because staff don't realise they're trans, because staff are prejudiced, or because well-meaning staff lack the training to behave appropriately. In some cases problems arise due to hostility or inappropriate behaviour on the part of other patients.

People with chronic illnesses sometimes have to pay multiple visits to hospital every year, even if they're only in for a few days at a time. This makes it especially important that they feel comfortable and safe there. In some cases, individual patient plans are able to be worked out in order to make visits as straightforward and stress-free as possible. The majority of problems arise when trans people have to deal with staff who have not had the chance to get to know them.

In England, each NHS Trust has its own policy on accommodating trans patients.

Choosing the right ward

Most trans men and women find it distressing to be placed on a ward other than the one appropriate to their gender. For non-binary people, such wards are usually unavailable, especially as mixed-sex wards are being phased out in NHS hospitals. Often it's not possible to provide individual rooms for patients in this situation, especially in the case of unplanned admissions. How should the situation be managed?

Single-sex wards

As a rule, trans people should always be accommodated on wards appropriate for their gender – trans women on women's wards and trans men on men's wards. There are, however, exceptions to this:

- In some cases, trans people prefer to be accommodated on wards associated with their birth-assigned gender. This can happen when, for instance, a trans man feels that he would be unsafe on a men's ward.

- Where treatments relate to sex-specific body parts and only one type of ward is available, such as when a trans man is having a hysterectomy.

Decisions about where to place a trans person should not be based on that person's appearance or their genitals, which staff should not ask about unless the information is medically relevant. The use of curtains should be sufficient to ensure privacy.

Non-binary people

When dealing with non-binary people, it's best to ask upfront what type of ward they would be most comfortable on. Although many prefer single rooms in the absence of mixed accommodation, this isn't always the case, so it shouldn't be assumed even in situations where such rooms can easily be made available. For some people, being in company is more important than being in an appropriate gender-segregated space.

For most non-binary people, being on a male ward or a female ward – even when they have chosen which – will always be an uncomfortable experience. This means it's important to talk with them about ways that it can be made easier. Bear in mind that they may not want you to take measures that make their gender apparent to other patients on the ward. Some people are most comfortable living openly all the time, but others prefer to avoid the risk of encountering transphobia, especially in situations where they're already feeling vulnerable.

Trans and gender-questioning children

Research increasingly supports the notion that allowing children to express their gender even when it doesn't conform to standard expectations is important to their mental health.[80] This may involve providing puberty blockers at the appropriate stage in development. In younger children, it is normally focused on changing name, pronouns and presentation. In a hospital environment this means that a child should be treated as a member of their self-identified gender, including in situations where wards are segregated. There is no evidence that this places other children at risk. Staff should be aware of the potential for bullying if other children find out that a child is trans, however, and should also be aware that adults can become aggressive towards children in this situation.

When you're unsure

If a patient who appears to be trans is admitted when unconscious or otherwise unable to communicate, and if there is no one else present who can be asked where they would be most comfortable, it's best to make a decision about where to place them based on aspects of personal presentation such as dress. As soon as you get a chance to speak to them, you can explain where they are and explain that they were placed where space was available and that you can move them if they would prefer to be on a different ward.

Addressing the situation in this way reduces the risk that they will be offended if their gender has been misinterpreted.

You should always be aware that a carer or family member accompanying a trans person to hospital may not know that they are trans, or may be hostile if they do know, so there is always a risk that you will be given incorrect information. The patient's own expressed wishes should always take priority.

You can apply a similar approach with patients who are able to communicate if you think they might be trans or non-binary, simply by explaining where you're going to put them and asking if they're comfortable with that. Joking that nobody feels completely comfortable about going into hospital can help to alleviate any tension. It can be helpful to take this approach, as gently as possible, with patients who simply seem withdrawn or depressed, giving them as much opportunity as possible to express their needs – obviously, gender-related discomfort is just one issue that can come up in this situation. If you have clear signals that the hospital is an LGBT-friendly environment, such as posters with LGBT rainbow motifs on the walls, it can make patients feel more confident about speaking up.

Some trans people are really scared by the thought of being taken into hospital in an emergency, because of the lack of control they would have over the situation and the prospect of facing transphobia, to the point where they avoid activities such as sports for fear of having accidents. This obviously has negative health outcomes. It demonstrates how important it is to be reassuring and create a space that feels safe.

Issues with staff

In order to avoid issues arising with staff expressing prejudiced views or discriminating against trans patients, it is vital to ensure that everybody who comes into contact with patients has appropriate training. This means not only doctors, nurses and therapists but also receptionists, pharmacists, porters and cleaners. Trans people need to know that they will be safe when they go into hospital, and what may seem like minor transgressions can have a serious effect on people who have a high chance of having experienced bullying or assault in connection with transphobic prejudice in the past.

Discrimination sometimes takes subtle forms. It isn't all a matter of inappropriate remarks. Trans patients frequently report that they are neglected by staff. Many may not even be aware that this is happening because they don't know how often nurses should be checking on them, for instance, but in some circumstances it could put them in danger. Staff may refuse to provide non-medical support services such as fetching wheelchairs when they need to move between rooms or offering cups of tea when other patients are receiving them.

Staff members whose behaviour risks making patients feel unsafe need to be kept away from those patients – potentially by being transferred to another department – until the matter is able to be dealt with. This often means being provided with additional training. In some cases, however, all that's needed is a talk focused on helping them to understand why their behaviour is problematic and how it affects patient well-being.

It's important to be aware that transphobia can have a negative effect on more people than just individual openly trans patients. There may be other patients or members of staff present who are trans but have not come out. There may also be people with trans loved ones who experience anxiety when reminded of the hostile attitudes that could place those people at risk. Gay, lesbian and bisexual patients and staff members may worry that people who are hostile towards trans people could also be hostile towards them.

Neglect stemming from transphobia can put a strain on other members of staff as they try to fill in the gaps.

Issues with patients

In general, hospital patients have bigger things to worry about than who they are sharing a ward with, and they are more likely to complain about disruptive patients than about anyone quiet. Trans people are rarely disruptive because they usually try to avoid drawing attention to themselves. In some cases, however, you may encounter a patient who objects to the presence of a trans person on the same ward. In accordance with the provisions of the Equality Act (2010) you should try to resolve the situation through education. Talk to the worried patient and ask precisely what they're worried about. Reassure them that curtains will be used to ensure privacy and that staff will always be nearby so they are not in any danger, and explain that trans women are not likely to hurt anyone anyway. It can be helpful to discuss how they feel about the treatment they are in for, and explain that the trans patient will have similar worries or will be feeling similarly unwell. Try to encourage empathy.

If worries persist, try to move the worried patient to the other end of the ward or closer to the nurses' station. Don't move the trans patient, who should not be held responsible for other people's prejudice or misunderstanding.

If another patient threatens or harasses a trans patient, deal with it as you would any other incident of aggression. Reassure the trans person that you don't share the aggressor's prejudice and that you will not tolerate such behaviour. Even comparatively minor incidents should not go unchallenged in case they escalate.

Issues with visitors

Often the people who cause the most trouble on wards are visitors, who may feel that by doing so they are defending their loved ones' interests. This can be particularly distressing not just for trans people but for other people who are on the same ward and really don't want to be caught up in a hostile situation. It's important to intervene quickly in situations like this to prevent escalation. Be clear that you don't allow abusive language or threatening behaviour. If problems persist, you can suggest that the visitors meet the patient they are coming to see in the day room instead of on the ward. If you are still concerned about their behaviour towards the trans patient (whether this takes the form of direct hostility or passive-aggressive comments made with the intention that they are overheard), you will have to ask them to leave. The target of abusive behaviour should never be the one who is asked to move elsewhere.

Handing over care

If a trans person has been admitted on your shift and you are about to hand over to the next shift, or if you are arranging for a trans person to be moved to another unit, should you explain that they are trans? Wherever possible, this is something that you should discuss with the patient before the situation arises. If they agree, it's best to raise the issue just so that they don't have to go through it all again with somebody else. Make sure that it's clear you're raising it because you want to ensure that the patient is supported, and that your words don't come across as gossip or a warning.

Having a discussion like this gives you that chance to look out for any signs of prejudice in your replacement that may jeopardise the care the patient receives. If you are concerned, speak to somebody else who will be present and ask them to keep an eye on the situation.

In theatre

Theatre technicians often see patients only briefly and in conditions where hair is covered, any make-up has been removed and there are no personal effects to signal gender. Nevertheless, it is important that they know when a patient is trans, for two reasons. First, it can affect the choice of drugs to be used (this is something that should be discussed before the procedure begins but it's important to keep it in focus in case complications necessitate quick decision-making). Second, they may participate in the process of soothing the patient before anaesthesia and talking to them during any break in anaesthesia, and avoiding misgendering in the situation is essential if the patient is to remain relaxed.

When patients enter the recovery room, it's important to make sure that staff know how to address them appropriately. If a trans woman normally wears a wig, replacing it for her while she's still unconscious can reduce the risk of misgendering and make her feel more confident and comfortable as she comes round. You shouldn't try to replace binders used by trans men for privacy reasons and because they can restrict breathing at a point where it's risky to do so because the effects of anaesthetic haven't fully worn off. However, providing an extra blanket and keeping it loose on top of the bed can make it easier for them to disguise the shape of breasts, again making it easier to feel confident when waking up in a room full of strangers.

Instances have been reported of trans people being addressed by their birth names when coming round after surgery, with well-meaning staff doing this because they think it will help with recognition. On the contrary, it is likely to lead to confusion and distress. Even people who have only just come out as trans have often privately identified themselves with their new names for a long time, and the relief experienced upon being able to use such a name publicly ensures that there's no possibility of it being forgotten. Using the name a trans patient has chosen provides immediate reassurance that they are respected and are in a safe environment.

Practical issues

There are some commonplace hospital procedures that need extra thought where trans people are concerned.

Bed sheets

Trans men and non-binary people who have had breasts removed may have a lot of sensitivity, or even chronic pain, in the chest area. In this situation they are unlikely to be able to sleep under tightly tucked bed sheets, so standard procedures should be relaxed.

Bedpans

In most circumstances, unless you are directly involved in looking after a trans patient's genital health, it's not appropriate to ask what their genitals look like. When supporting a bedbound trans patient who needs to urinate, it's best to default to supplying bedpans regardless of gender, and asking discretely if a urinal would be more appropriate. Carrying a urinal to and from a trans woman or feminine non-binary person's bed might inadvertently disclose their transness to other patients, so this should be avoided if possible and otherwise done discreetly.

Catheterisation

If a trans man is being fitted with a catheter, extra care should be taken to avoid harm, whatever the shape of his genitals. An extended urethra inside a constructed penis is more fragile than that in a typical penis. Even in trans men who have not had genital surgery, the skin around the genitals is often thinner than usual due to the effects of testosterone. The same issue can apply with some non-binary people, so try to find out if they are taking testosterone first.

Do not resuscitate (DNR) notices

Many disabled people are afraid that, when they go into hospital, they will be subject to DNR notices because of an assumption that their quality of life is so poor that it would be wrong to resuscitate them if they should stop breathing. For trans disabled people, this is even more worrying due to the common assumption that trans lives are tragic and unhappy. In fact, many trans disabled people are quite happy with their quality of life, which they have fought very hard to achieve.

DNR notices should never be issued without consent. Some patients may need reassurance that no such notice has been added to their notes, especially if they have experienced hostility from members of staff.

12

Institutional Care

Where hospital is unnecessary but day-to-day difficulties are severe or at-home care is unavailable, trans people may need institutional care. As with other people, this becomes more likely over the life course. Because people only began transitioning in significant numbers around 30–40 years ago, and because transition over the age of 60 was rare at that stage, it is only now that significant numbers of trans people are beginning to enter institutional care, as severe disability is much more common in later life. This means that institutions are undergoing a rapid process of adjustment to try to accommodate trans people's needs.

Nowhere is it more important to provide a safe, respectful environment than in the home. When an institution becomes home, it is vital that residents feel secure and able to be themselves. Improving your understanding of trans people's experiences and needs can help your institution to achieve that.

Creating a safe space

Do you have trans people resident in your institution? You might assume that you don't, but think again – are you *sure*? It's not always easy to tell, because people may try to hide their transness in situations like this if they don't feel safe. Of course, if they have happily transitioned and simply don't feel any need to mention their past, and this doesn't create any problems with the particular kind of medical support they need, that's not a problem. If they have reverted to living in their assigned gender, however, it could mean that they are suffering from severe dysphoria, with a negative effect on their wider health.

In addition to this, some people come out as trans for the first time when they enter institutional care. There are two major reasons for this. First, it's a break with the past and this provides a chance to re-evaluate life and reset personal priorities. Second, they may be confronted by a much more gendered lifestyle than they have been used to (from the terms staff use to address them to the decor used in private rooms), and this can precipitate a crisis wherein dysphoria that has previously been mild becomes much stronger.

People who are not trans can also experience gender-related stress that is alleviated when a strongly gender-related approach is relaxed. Many men and women who are comfortable identifying with the genders they were assigned at birth still feel uncomfortable if they are expected to be macho or very feminine, yet may feel uncomfortable saying so because they worry about not fitting in socially.

Shared spaces

Shared spaces in institutions need to feel safe to all residents. Most staff are already aware of the need to clamp down on racist language used by residents, and the same approach should be taken when it comes to transphobia. Residents can be as unpleasant as they like in their own rooms, but no resident should feel unable to enter a shared space for fear of encountering hostility.

Naturally, this can become difficult if some of your residents have impaired cognition or self-control, because of the effects of a stroke, for instance. When managing situations like this, you should always give priority consideration to the person who is facing abuse. This may mean that you have to work out an arrangement limiting the hours when an abusive resident is allowed to use the shared space. You should let any new trans resident know that this is an ongoing behavioural issue and not something they need to take personally. They are likely to cope much better if you show (not just tell) them that you are on their side.

Some other residents may have misgivings about trans people simply due to lack of experience. In some cases, a new openly trans resident may be happy to engage in a question-and-answer session to resolve concerns where possible and start building positive connections. In other cases they may feel uncomfortable about this or simply feel that it's no one's business to ask them to explain or justify who they are. If they don't want to engage like this and you're worried that long-term problems may develop, look up local trans organisations and see if they can help you find another trans person who is happy to come in and talk.

You may find that none of your residents are bothered by the presence of a trans person. This is a more common situation than most people realise, so don't feel that you have an obligation to raise the subject if everybody seems to be getting along fine.

If you have a resident who has transitioned and is not open about it, it's important to keep the matter confidential. It's not your place to expose people's gender history without their consent.

Just as you should manage the behaviour of residents in shared spaces, you should be careful about television and radio broadcasts in such spaces. This is especially important when you're dealing with residents who cannot move around unaided. No trans person should ever be stuck in a room where hostile rhetoric about trans people is being broadcast.

Being flexible about family

Because many trans people experience a breakdown in their relationships with family members, they may develop close bonds with people who they are not related to by blood or marriage but who are just as important to them as parents, siblings and children are to others. This makes it important for care homes to have visitor policies that are flexible and don't restrict access to only those people traditionally thought of as family members, even in situations where an individual is very ill. A best friend may be the most important person in that individual's life, and the person best placed to provide emotional support.

When an individual enters institutional care for the first time, it is, of course, important to make a note of their next of kin. What many people don't realise, however, is that their next of kin can be anybody – they don't have to be blood relatives. Explaining this can help people who may have experienced family breakdown to make better choices about who oversees their care in the event of them being unable to do so themselves. If they cannot think of anybody suitable, you can suggest that they nominate a solicitor who will then act in accordance with instructions they have prepared in advance.

Family secrets

Sometimes family members visiting a trans person will be doing so in secret because of family rifts over that person's transition. This means that it's important for staff to avoid gossiping about who has been visiting, even to other visitors. The fact that a visit occurs doesn't necessarily mean that family member is supportive. For instance, an estranged son may visit his trans mother to discuss legacy issues, but feel betrayed if he finds out that his sister has been maintaining a close relationship with her. Although it might be tempting to try to persuade family members to reunite, this is an area in which the resident should always be the one taking the lead. The most helpful thing you can do is to show that you respect their gender and don't feel any prejudice towards them.

Because trans residents may not be out to all their family members, it's important to ask them if there's anyone they'd prefer you to keep in the dark. This could mean you having to remember to use a different name and pronouns when talking about them to some people, and it could mean that they need to change their clothes before certain visitors arrive, but making that effort could be a big help in enabling them to maintain a happy family life. It can be handled in a similar way to situations in which residents don't want their relatives to know that their health is getting worse.

Family hostility

In some cases you may encounter people who are angry that their relative is being allowed to live in their preferred gender role in your institution. This is most common in situations where that person was not open about being trans before. Sometimes relatives will try to have a person in this situation moved to another institution, arguing that they are not mentally competent to make the decision to live that way by themselves. This is a particular risk in situations where the resident's mental capacities are compromised to some degree – for example, by dementia.

In cases like this it can help to direct the complainant to books or online resources where they can learn more about trans people. If other residents are accepting of the trans person, you can show that living that way is not having negative consequences and explain that your priority is to make sure residents feel happy and are able to express themselves as they wish. Often, strong initial objections will give way to a slow process of acceptance. You might suggest family counselling as a means of helping all involved to come to terms with the situation. Pink Therapy maintains a searchable database of LGBTI-friendly counsellors,[81] including individuals with specific expertise in helping trans people and their families.

Residents with trans visitors

Staff providing institutional care may also encounter trans people when they arrive as visitors, coming to see their relatives. In the past, such visitors were often discouraged, either purely as a result of prejudice or out of concern that they might upset or confuse elderly or vulnerable residents. Today such discouragement would potentially breach the Equality Act, and, furthermore, the number of such visitors who have been able to see their loved ones has demonstrated that this is unlikely to cause significant problems (bearing in mind that clashes can exist within any family). As a rule, people who expect clashes don't want to visit.

Even where a resident experiences cognitive decline, coping with the fact that a relative has changed gender role does not seem to be any more confusing than other aspects of life. In October 2015, Tina Healy, a care worker and an advocate for Gender Diversity Australia, revealed that she has explained her transition to her mother, who has dementia, on multiple occasions, and that each time the response is delight.[82]

Residents with transphobic visitors

If people enter your institution as visitors, they should follow the same rules as residents when they're in shared spaces, and should treat everybody respectfully and avoid using prejudiced language. Visitors who don't follow these rules should be restricted to visits in private rooms, escorted to and from them by a member of staff, or – if even this proves problematic – banned from visiting. In some cases it may be possible to arrange for visits to take place in the grounds outside, instead.

Practical issues

There are some practical issues for trans people living in institutional care that you will need to be aware of.

If you have people in your institution who do not wish to be open about the fact that they're trans, you will need to think carefully about procedures for managing medication. This is because some trans men need medication that other residents will associate with women, while some trans women need medication that other residents will associate with men – something that can potentially out them. If they store their medication in their rooms, make sure they can do so discreetly. If medicine is handed out to residents as needed, make sure that packaging is not visible to other residents and that the names of medicines are not spoken too loudly or called across the room. If you see this simply as part of the privacy that ought to be due to every patient, you might be surprised to learn how often it's overlooked.

Trans women who have had genital reconstructive surgery to create a vagina often need to make regular use of a dilator in order to keep the vagina from shrinking. This is especially important during the first few months and years after surgery, but it sometimes remains necessary throughout the life course. It is most easily done in a hot bath. If it isn't possible to provide a bath, a trans woman living in care will, at the very least, need access to a private room in which to carry out this procedure. As it works best when the body is relaxed, it's easiest when the mind is relaxed too, so it's best if this is her bedroom. Wherever it is, she will need to be able to be 100% confident that she will not be interrupted. If her disability means that she needs a nurse to help with the procedure, discretion should be exercised regarding the reason for the nurse's visit.

13

At-Home Care

Trans people who receive care in their own homes require special consideration. They are less likely to receive kinship care or have an extended support network. They may have had bad experiences with professional carers and be wary about interacting with new ones. They may also struggle to find carers who understand their specific needs.

Kinship care

Where trans people receive kinship care, additional complications can be present on top of the issues common to this situation.

Intimate relationships often – though not universally – become non-sexual after transition, and this can complicate the provision of intimate care. One partner may continue to feel attracted whereas the other does not, or a non-transitioning partner may find it distressing to interact directly with the parts of their partner's body that have changed. This can apply even where a strong romantic relationship remains. The result can be that general care is good but intimate care is inadequate, or that the provision of intimate care is causing ongoing, potentially cumulative stress to one or both partners.

Kinship carers who want to be supportive but struggle to come to terms with the cared-for person's transition may need support themselves. There is advice available[83] to help with this, and support groups[84] through which it's possible to meet other people with similar experiences. It's also worth thinking about family counselling as an option.

Abuse and neglect

Research conducted by the Scottish Transgender Alliance in 2013 found that trans people experience high levels of domestic abuse, especially emotional abuse related to their gender.[85] Given that disabled people already face elevated levels of domestic abuse,[86] this is of particular concern, and health and care professionals working with trans people who receive kinship care should be alert to possible signs of abuse, including neglect.

In some situations, trans people are cared for by family members who do not respect their gender. This can make it difficult for them to express themselves appropriately through their clothing and personal grooming, and it sometimes impedes their access to trans-related support services. In a situation like this, it might not always be apparent to the heath or care workers they come into contact with that they are trans. Little things like having a poster about LGBT support services on an office wall or having a rainbow ribbon attached to your bag can signpost you as a safe person to talk to if help is needed. As always, if you suspect that a disabled person might not feel able to speak freely in the presence of their carer, you should ask to speak to them alone.

Young people

Young people face additional challenges in coming out to family members as trans if they are disabled and dependent on those family members for care. Although there are no figures currently available on the rejection of trans children and young people by their families, the Albert Kennedy Trust has found that LGBT people make up a disproportionately high part of the homeless community, with 77% of them saying that the main reason for their homelessness is familial rejection.[87] As noted in their report, this may involve physical or sexual abuse. Young disabled people may fear that they could not survive this or that they would have nowhere to go. They may also see institutional care as the only alternative to remaining in the familial home, and fear that this would close down all their opportunities in life.

Mermaids[88] and Gendered Intelligence[89] provide support for young trans people and can be useful points of contact in finding ways to deal with this situation.

Some researchers have suggested that GPs should find opportunities to ask all adolescent patients if they have any concerns about gender issues that they feel the need to talk about, thereby reducing the risk that those in need will fail to ask for help.[90]

Living 'in stealth mode'

Sometimes adult trans people are cared for by relatives who don't know that they're trans. They may not feel safe to come out or they may not wish to do so because they believe it would cause distress, especially if the carer is an ageing parent. This doesn't mean, however, that they will be comfortable concealing their gender all the time. This is a situation in which respite care can be as important for the cared-for person as for the carer. Even getting a break once a week to go to a trans support group under the pretence of doing something else can make a big difference to their mental health and general well-being.

Access to the internet can be especially important for people in this situation. Many prefer to access it through their phones or other mobile devices rather than through shared household computers, so carers should make sure that they are able to access such devices and keep them charged.

Care agencies

Care agencies are bound by the Equality Act and have a duty to ensure that their staff don't discriminate or express prejudice against their trans clients. This means that they need to provide appropriate training, be ready to follow up quickly on any concerns, and avoid sending staff members to assist trans clients if they have any reason to believe that those staff members may behave inappropriately. They also need to be aware that clients who feel vulnerable may hesitate to report problems, and take proactive measures to check that there are no issues with the care they are receiving. Any request by a trans person to change carer or have a particular carer removed from their rota should be treated seriously, even if it is difficult to determine the existence of any prejudice or discrimination.

In many cases, carers will not have any reason to know whether or not a client is trans, and this should not be raised as an 'issue' unless the client wants it to happen – for instance, as an additional means of ensuring that they don't have to deal with prejudiced carers. In other situations, depending on the anatomy of the client and the type of care needed, it may not be possible to avoid the carer knowing. The client should have the final word in any discussion of how best to handle this, but in general it is better to ensure that there will be no surprises, as those are the situations in which there is the greatest risk of prejudice or outright hostility being expressed.

Because the possibility of having to deal with prejudice makes every encounter with a new carer additionally stressful for a trans client, aiming for consistency in terms of who is sent to provide care is particularly important.

Opening Doors London advises that care agencies publish a demographic profile of their own staff[91] so they can tell what proportions of different minorities are represented within the group. Although no staff member should be obliged to share personal details for this reason, it can help with internal equality monitoring and it also means that – without private details about any individual staff member being shared inappropriately – clients can immediately see that the carers they are sent could be from the same minority groups as themselves or that they could have colleagues from those groups, so they won't be so worried about facing prejudice. It also notes that getting positive stories about an agency into the LGBT press means that LGBT people may feel more confident about approaching it.

Partnering with a local trans organisation or a fully trans-inclusive LGBT organisation can be a good way to improve your agency's capacity. You will be able to turn to the group for advice and potentially refer trans clients to it for support. It may refer new clients to you. You may be able to provide it with advice on how to make its activities more accessible to disabled people.

Caring for trans people's specific needs

In order to live with the same level of comfort and dignity as their peers, trans people may need specific kinds of help that differ from the needs of other people with disabilities or chronic illnesses. Caring for a trans man is not always the same as caring for a cis man, and caring for a trans woman is not always the same as caring for a cis woman. The experiences of non-binary people vary but learning how to support trans men and women can make it easier to work out how to assist them in accordance with their stated needs.

Binding

If they have not had breast removal surgery, most trans men prefer to use a binder in order to flatten the chest area. This may matter to them only when they're going out of the house or it may be something that they need every day in order to maintain good mental health. Although there can be physical health issues associated with binding, these are not a major issue for everyone and many disabled trans men do it routinely. It may not, however, be something they can do for themselves. Pulling a binder into position requires quite a bit of strength and positioning it correctly requires a good degree of flexibility in the shoulders, elbows and wrists.

If you need to help somebody fit a binder, follow his instructions carefully to make sure he's as comfortable as possible. The binder (which looks like a tight vest) should normally go on over the feet, inside out and upside down, so if the wearer can't stand comfortably, the easiest way to fit it is usually on a bed where it can be wriggled into, turning back and forth to slide it over the hips in stages. Once it reaches the waist it can be folded over so that it turns the right way round as it's pulled up. If arm movement is limited, the hands should be inserted into the arm holes as early as possible so that arms can remain straight as it's pulled into position. The breasts will be pushed upwards naturally as the binder is tugged into place, and they should be moved outwards – towards the armpits – for the best flattening effect.

Some trans men bind using tape or bandages, but there are serious health risks associated with this. If you find yourself asked to help with this, support the individual's wishes but ask if he would be willing to wear a binder instead and if he needs help to get hold of one.

Unless your client requests otherwise, always talk about the chest rather than the breasts when discussing this process, as some trans men find the latter distressing.

Menstruation

Coping with menstruation can be a sensitive issue for any disabled person who needs a high degree of personal care. Many trans men menstruate, and for them the experience can be complicated by dysphoria.

Like women, trans men adopt a variety of solutions to manage menstruation at a practical level. Some prefer options that minimise the frequency with which they have to think about the process, whereas others prefer options that mean they don't have to deal with any form of vaginal penetration. Because of the complexity of the sensitivities involved, it is important that they are not put in a position where they have to switch away from the option they feel most comfortable with.

Something that many trans men find particularly difficult is the process of buying sanitary protection, especially if they are young and shopkeepers are less likely to assume that they're buying it for somebody else. If you're helping with shopping, it can be useful to take an extra bag to give the impression that some of what you're buying is for your client and some is for you or your family. Don't make a fuss – just be relaxed and follow your client's lead. Most people, if they notice what you're buying at all, will jump to familiar conclusions before considering anything more unusual.

Hair removal

Some trans women have ongoing problems with facial hair and need regular treatment sessions in order to remove it. The most popular treatment option for hair removal is electrolysis, but in order for this to be effective, a full growth of stubble needs to be present before the session commences. This can cause dysphoria and serious social difficulties. Carers who help a client in this situation with personal grooming should be aware that they can use burn cream or a similar heavy ointment as a base for make-up to conceal stubble. It rarely looks completely natural but most trans women feel that it looks a lot better than the alternative.

After electrolysis treatment, skin is usually raw and very sensitive, comparable to a bad sunburn. Burn cream can also be useful at this stage, for protecting the skin and easing pain. A simple, unscented moisturiser makes a good alternative.

When problems with stubborn facial hair are less severe, home electrolysis is also an option, and this can be a practical choice for people whose health issues make it difficult for them to attend appointments. Home electrolysis kits are simple to use but it is important not to exceed the recommended time limit for exposure, even if the client asks you to. Damage caused by prolonged exposure may not immediately be apparent.

Dressing trans people

Many trans people find that the clothes they want to wear are not usually designed for people with their body type. This is as much the case for non-binary people as it is for trans men and trans women. Clothes designed to create an androgynous appearance tend not to account for characteristics like large breasts or bulky muscle.

When combined with disability issues that limit mobility, this can make it particularly difficult to find suitable clothes that fit well and are easy to get on and off. People who experience progressive disability may gradually compromise on clothes to the point where their dysphoria gets worse because they simply cannot achieve an appearance that reflects their gender or conceals the most prominent signs of the wrong gender. It can help to discuss clothes with clients, especially when they are new to receiving care, to find out if better arrangements can be made. This might include having clothes specially modified so that they can be put on in pieces and then reassembled, such as suit jackets with hidden fastenings along the back seam. Adaptive clothing designed to accommodate common disabilities is available from several different companies, but many disabled people don't realise that these exist.

Non-binary people

It's important not to make assumptions about non-binary people's gender-related needs. Staff should be aware that even if they look typically male or female, this doesn't mean that they will feel comfortable being treated that way – disability can make it difficult for people to present themselves as they would ideally like to and some people feel that they shouldn't have to dress a certain way in order to be respected for who they are. Gendered terms like 'good boy' and 'good girl' should be avoided even in situations where a client is in pain or experiencing distress and needs reassurance and comfort. These are, in fact, often the times at which people find it most difficult to cope with being misgendered.

Toilet access

Helping a client to get out and about in public spaces can include helping them to access public toilets. Although most disabled toilets are gender-neutral, some are positioned within larger blocks of men's or women's toilets. Some disabled people who do need assistance to get around don't need to use an adapted toilet – people with visual impairments, for instance, can usually manage perfectly well in a standard toilet but may need somebody to take them to the door of the stall.

In this situation, it's important to take your client to the toilets that they feel are most appropriate to their gender. Most (but not all) non-binary people feel safer using women's toilets when forced to choose, because of the expectation that transphobic women may be threatening but transphobic men are more likely to be physically aggressive. You should note that there are no laws in the UK restricting toilet access by gender. This has only ever been a matter of custom. An individual behaving in an inappropriate manner in toilets associated with a different sex could be committing a breach of the peace, but there is no law that stops anyone from simply being there and using them for the purpose for which they are intended.

Most of the time, trans people using public toilets do not face hostility, so you should not be overly worried about this. If you are challenged and your client looks to you for help, simply explain that they have a right to be there and that they are not posing a danger to anybody. Never apologise for taking your client in there unless doing so is essential to staying physically safe.

Some trans people take incidents like this in their stride and are not seriously bothered by them. Others may feel badly shaken and need to go somewhere quiet afterwards to recover from the immediate effects of the experience.

14

Transgender People, Disability Benefits and Financial Issues

Like many other people living with disability or chronic illness, trans people in this situation may need disability benefits in order to get by day to day. They can face additional barriers in accessing these. It's common for them to be living below the poverty line and this can complicate aspects of their access to medical treatment as well as contributing to poor physical and mental health outcomes.

Prejudice and discrimination

Claiming state benefits is already an experience that many people find humiliating.[92] For trans people, it can be made worse by the experience of prejudice or discrimination, either from staff or from other claimants. Unless an individual is so severely incapacitated that home visits are required, interacting with the benefits system is done through job centres, which frequently have large and crowded waiting rooms and which are mostly open plan in design, making it difficult to avoid being visible to strangers and in some cases making it difficult to talk without the risk of being overheard.

Even if sensitive details are not required as part of a given interview, trans people risk being identified as trans if their voices don't match people's expectations in relation to their appearance. They may also be identified because of the way they look. This places them at risk of transphobic abuse in a situation where many people are under stress and tempers are often frayed.

Staff attitudes to trans people are generally considered to have improved a great deal over the past decade, and few trans people have raised concerns, even with their peers, about clear instances of prejudice coming from staff. Research for this book revealed, however, that some believe they may have been discriminated against in subtler ways as a result of transphobic prejudice. This is difficult to prove, but it's clear that there is the potential for abuse, especially because the need to satisfy representatives of the benefits system in order to access money needed for basic necessities puts claimants in a precarious position in which they can find it difficult to assert their rights.

Expectations of prejudice

Prejudice doesn't even need to be demonstrated in order to present a problem. Many trans people have long histories of negative experiences when interacting with service providers, or have heard distressing stories from other trans people. This can make them shy away from such interactions or delay them until their circumstances have become desperate.

Medical professionals and caregivers can help with this by stressing that many trans people successfully interact with the benefits system without encountering prejudice, and by emphasising the importance of starting claims for support as early as possible because they may take some time to process. Where possible, caregivers should offer to accompany the trans people they support to appointments, even if practical assistance is not needed. DWP staff are required to accept the presence of a carer if the claimant gives permission for them to be there.

Safeguarding measures

Unfortunately, measures like these can create problems in themselves. Where only a limited number of people are permitted to access a claimant's records, there can be delays in getting claims processed. If a claim is suspended for any reason – for instance, because there's uncertainty about how much money a claimant is making from self-employment or because an appointment has been missed (both common scenarios for disabled people) – then there can be delays in restarting it, potentially leaving people with no income. This is a particularly serious problem for trans people because there is a significant risk that they will be estranged from their families and have no one to turn to for help.

At present, there does not appear to be any mechanism through which a trans person in this situation can give temporary or permanent permission for their records to be accessed by a different person – the restrictions remain even if they would prefer them not to. Although this does remove the risk of claimants being placed in a position where they feel pressured to compromise their privacy (and potentially their safety), it also means that there is nothing they can do to expedite claims delayed as a result of safeguarding.

Problems can also arise because the majority of DWP staff are not aware that blocks on accessing data about particular service users can be legitimate. In at least one case, the police have been called in because the staff involved assumed that the claim must be fraudulent.

The DWP and transition

People wishing to change their details with the DWP when they transition need to supply a deed poll or statutory declaration to confirm change of name, and a doctor's letter to confirm that they have transitioned (this does not need to involve hormones or surgery; it simply needs to confirm that the transition is serious). On this basis they will change name, title and pronouns. Although individual experiences vary, DWP staff are generally fairly good at addressing people appropriately, including non-binary people. They will not, however, change gender in their systems unless a gender recognition certificate has been issued.

A gender recognition certificate entitles the holder to a new National Insurance card with their new name details on it. There is a policy of only ever issuing one replacement card in a lifetime, however, so no further ones are available for future name changes or even to replace a lost card.

Poverty and the challenges of saving money

Disabled people are significantly more likely than members of the general population to live below the poverty line.[93] This can make transition more difficult for them as they are unlikely to be able to afford procedures not available on the NHS, such as surgery to modify the voice or to change the shape of the face. This is even more difficult if they are dependent on benefits, because the DWP only allows claimants to save a limited amount of money before money starts to be subtracted from the weekly amount they receive in benefits. At the time of writing, the threshold is £6000, which is too low an amount to cover some such procedures, especially if travel is involved, and especially in light of the additional costs that many disabled people have, such as the need to pay for accessible transport and the need to pay for a carer.

The upshot of this situation is that many disabled people find themselves permanently unable to access treatments that could enable them to complete a satisfactory transition and improve their quality of life.

The high cost of being trans and disabled

Being disabled is expensive. Being trans is expensive. Being both can make life extremely difficult, forcing many people into poverty. Key issues include the following:

- **Having to travel long distances to see gender specialists.** Aside from the physical strain it often causes, this can be very difficult for those disabled people who need somebody to accompany them. Disabled people's rail cards do not cover the full cost of travel for a carer.

- **Having to live somewhere that is accessible and safe.** Often sheltered housing and housing designed for those with mobility difficulties is located in areas where average education levels are low and, correspondingly, levels of prejudice are high.[94]

- **Having to pay for things because there's no one to help.** Many trans people have no positive family relationships and few friends, so if they can't do household jobs themselves and those are not suitable tasks for carers, they have to pay every time.

These increased day-to-day costs often leave trans people with very little disposable income, reducing social opportunities still further.

In recognition of all this, carers should be thoughtful about the activities they suggest to trans clients, and should let them take the lead in such discussions as much as possible. Doctors, physiotherapists and other medical staff should be realistic when suggesting complementary therapies, dietary changes or activities that could be financially impossible.

Afterword

In light of this lengthy exploration of the challenges that disabled trans people face, it seems necessary to say a few words about other aspects of their lives that medical and care professionals may overlook.

Although it's true that there is a high incidence of depression, anxiety and suicidal ideation in this group, that does not mean that disabled trans people's lives are all doom and gloom. Many have jobs that they love, families they remain close to, happy romantic relationships and busy social lives. Where they have managed to transition in the way they hoped for, they are often able to put many of their problems behind them and enjoy a renewed lease of life. There are disabled trans people who have become successful scientists, creative artists, business leaders and politicians. Nobody should ever be written off because of the challenges they face.

Good, supportive work from GPs, nurses, psychiatrists and other medical professionals can help to make the process of transition much easier and more accessible. Good work from carers can significantly increase life opportunities and general well-being.

This is not a book about people who inevitably live life as victims. Rather, it should evidence the way that aspects of society need to change so that disabled trans people are free to be their authentic selves – as capable and complicated and passionate and human as anybody else.

Appendix 1: Finding Out More

Where can you find out more about trans people? The following organisations can provide advice and support.

GIRES – the Gender Identity Research & Education Society collates research on important issues concerning trans people and can provide advice on best practice. www.gires.org.uk

Mermaids – a charity dedicated to supporting young trans people and their families, able to help with research and advise on the best way to assist young people who are questioning their gender. www.mermaidsuk.org.uk

The Scottish Trans Alliance (previously, the Scottish Transgender Alliance) – a charity supported by the Scottish government which carries out research, provides training and has an extensive collection of resources that can help you to understand many different aspects of trans people's lives. www.scottishtrans.org

Stonewall – a charity focused on LGBT rights which carries out research on trans people's experiences, and provides training. www.stonewall.org.uk

Information on trans people in healthcare environments

NHS England has its Gender Dysphoria Protocol on its website with help for healthcare professionals who need to refer patients to specialist gender services, plus information for GPs on how to prescribe and monitor hormones. www.nhs.uk/conditions/gender-dysphoria/guidelines

NHS Scotland has its Gender Reassignment Protocol on its website along with explanatory notes and additional guidance for healthcare professionals. www.ngicns.scot.nhs.uk/nhs-scotland-gender-reassignment-protocol-grp

NHS Wales details how trans patients should be supported in its Specialised Services Policy (CP21), which is available on its website. www.whssc.wales.nhs.uk/document/281109

The Royal College of Nursing has published a guide to *Fair care for trans patients* which is available upon request. www.rcn.org.uk

Exploring research on trans people

If you're looking for research on trans people, it's important to be aware that there's a lot of junk science on the subject which has been published and promoted by people who are ideologically opposed to trans people's existence. To ensure that you're not misled by this, take the same approach you would with any socially contested subject. Don't just rely on the first papers turned up by search engines to give you the facts. Stick to accredited, peer-reviewed journals. Examine the methodology in any study before deciding how much faith to place in its conclusions. If you're unsure about a theory, check to see if it's contested and ask suitably qualified friends or colleagues what they think of it.

Appendix 2: Glossary of Terms

Most people reading this book will find that it contains quite a bit of unfamiliar language. This glossary provides an easy way to check any words you're uncertain about.

agender *adj*. Having no gender, being outside the system of gender.

androgyne *adj., n*. (Person) having qualities of maleness and femaleness; usually used to refer to presentation.

assigned gender *n*. The gender formally associated with an individual at birth.

autogynephilia *n*. The theoretical state whereby a heterosexual man is sexually excited by imagining or presenting himself as female.

bigender *adj*. Having qualities of maleness and femaleness; used to refer to presentation or identity.

binary transgender *adj*. Pertaining to a man who was categorised as female at birth or a woman who was categorised as male at birth.

binary transition *n*. The process of transitioning from male to female or from female to male.

binder *n*. A garment worn by trans men and some non-binary people to flatten the chest area and reduce the appearance of breasts.

bottom surgery *n*. Surgery to change the appearance of the genitals, carried out as part of transition.

cis *adj*. Having a gender identity consistent with the way one was categorised at birth; short for *cisgender*.

cis man *n*. A man who was categorised as male at birth.

cis woman *n*. A woman who was categorised as female at birth.

cisgender *adj*. Having a gender identity consistent with the way one was categorised at birth.

cross-dress *v*. To wear clothing normally associated with a different gender; especially to dress in female-associated clothing if male.

detransition *v., n*. To reverse the social, hormonal or surgical aspect of a transition from one gender role to another; the process of undertaking such a reversal.

DSD *n*. An acronym for *disorders of sexual development* or *differences of sexual development* and referring to intersex variations.

dysphoria *n*. The state of feeling deeply uneasy or dissatisfied with life. Frequently used by trans people in reference to *gender dysphoria*.

fa'afafine *n*. A person from Samoa who is transfeminine and has a specific cultural role.

gender *n.* (1) The internal sense of being male, female or non-binary. (2) A term popularly used as a synonym for sex.

gender confirmation surgery *n.* A collective term for surgeries used to make a person's body more accurately reflect their gender; also, a term used to refer specifically to surgery used to make a person's genitals more accurately reflect their gender.

gender dysphoria *n.* The state of feeling deeply uneasy or dissatisfied with the gender role one is living in.

gender reassignment surgery *n.* Another term for *gender confirmation surgery*, now considered archaic and somewhat inaccurate.

gender role *n.* Presentation or behaviours culturally associated with a particular sex.

genderfluid *adj.* Experiencing different internal genders at different times; presenting in differently gendered ways at different times.

genderqueer *adj., n.* Having a gender identity that is not wholly or consistently male or female; a person whose gender identity is neither wholly nor consistently male or female.

hermaphrodite *adj., n.* Being born with a body that does not meet typical expectations of maleness or femaleness, or spontaneously developing a body that does not meet typical expectations of maleness or femaleness in adolescence; a stigmatising term which some people are trying to reclaim.

hijra *n.* A person from the Indian subcontinent who is either intersex or transfeminine and has a specific cultural role.

intergender *adj.* Having a gender identity that is between male and female.

intersex *adj.* Being born with a body which does not meet typical expectations of maleness or femaleness, or spontaneously developing a body which does not meet typical expectations of maleness or femaleness in adolescence.

LGBTI *n.* An acronym for lesbian, gay, bisexual, transgender and intersex.

mangina *n.* A trans man's vagina; a term sometimes used to reduce dysphoria when discussing genitals.

misgender *v.* To use incorrectly gendered pronouns or adjectives when describing somebody.

mx *n.* A non-gendered title equivalent to Mr or Ms.

neutrois *adj.* Identifying as neutrally gendered, neither male nor female.

non-binary *adj.* Having a gender identity that is not wholly or consistently male or female; an inoffensive umbrella term for genders that are neither male nor female.

non-gender *adj.* Not identifying with the concept of gender in relation to the self.

per *n.* A non-gendered title equivalent to Mr or Ms.

polygender *adj.* Having aspects of multiple genders.

retransition *v., n.* To undertake the process of transition again after having detransitioned; the process of going through a transition after having done so at least once previously.

sex *n.* Physiological maleness or femaleness or (sometimes, contentiously) the state of being intersex. There is no clear consensus on which characteristics should be given most weight when determining the sex of an individual.

shemale *n*. A person who has a penis and breasts. This term usually refers to someone who was categorised as male at birth. It is highly offensive and associated with pornography and sex work.

TERF *n*. An acronym for *trans exclusive radical feminist*, referring to a person (usually female) who identifies as a radical feminist and does not recognise trans women as women.

top surgery *n*. Surgery carried out on the chest area, usually to enhance, reduce or remove breasts.

tranny *n*. A trans woman or a transvestite. This is a heavily stigmatising term associated with pornography and sex work, but there is a significant movement to reclaim it for the purposes of self-identification.

trans *adj*. Short for transgender but frequently used on its own where the context is clear.

trans man *n*. A man who was categorised as female at birth.

trans woman *n*. A woman who was categorised as male at birth.

transfeminine *adj*. Descriptive of a trans woman or a non-binary person who leans in the direction of a feminine identity or presentation.

transgender *adj*. Having a gender identity inconsistent with the way one was categorised at birth. This term is also used in a narrower sense to refer specifically to people who have gone through a binary transition.

transgenderism *n*. An ideological position supportive of trans rights. This term is primarily used by people opposed to trans rights and should not be considered politically neutral.

transition *v*., *n*. To undergo the psychological, social, hormonal or surgical process of moving from life in one gender role to life in another; the undertaking of the psychological, social, hormonal or surgical process of moving from life in one gender role to life in another.

transmasculine *adj*. Descriptive of a trans man or a non-binary person who leans in the direction of a masculine identity or presentation.

transmisogyny *n*. Intersectional prejudice faced by trans women which combines elements of transphobia and misogyny.

transphobia *n*. Prejudice against trans people.

transexual *adj*. A person who is transitioning or has transitioned from male to female or from female to male. This term is sometimes considered inappropriate because it leads to easy confusion between gender and sexual orientation.

transvestite *n*., *adj*. A person who cross-dresses; sometimes also used as an adjective, as in, for example, a 'transvesite person'.

Pronouns

Several alternative pronouns are used by non-binary people in place of *he*, *she* and their derivatives. The following table details some of the most common ones, with more familiar examples to provide context.

Nominative	Accusative	Possessive adjective	Possessive pronoun	Reflexive
he	him	his	his	himself
she	her	her	hers	herself
they	them	their	theirs	themselves*
zie	zie	zir	zirs	zirself
xe	xe	xir	xirs	xirself
sie	hir	hir	hirs	hirself
per	per	per	pers	perself
fae	faer	faer	faers	faerself
co	co	co	cos	coself
ey	em	eir	eirs	emself

* Sometimes when *they* is used as a singular pronoun, the reflexive form *themself* is preferred.

The linguistic terms here might sound confusing but these pronouns are easy to use in practice. These examples show how the elements in the above table can be applied in simple sentences:

Nominative: There *she* is.

Accusative: Look at *her*.

Possessive adjective: That's *her* stick.

Possessive pronoun: That stick is *hers*.

Reflexive: She chose that stick for *herself*.

Endnotes

1   House of Commons Women and Equalities Committee (2016) *Transgender Equality: First Report of Session 2015–2016*. London: The Stationery Office. Accessed on 8/11/2018 at https://publications.parliament.uk/pa/cm201516/cmselect/cmwomeq/390/390.pdf.

2   The Wycliffe Bible (1382), Ecclus [Ecclesiastes] 38:35.

3   Butler, J. (1990) *Gender Trouble: Feminism and the Subversion of Identity*. Abingdon and New York, NY: Routledge.

4   Ruble, D.N., Taylor, L.J., Cyphers, L., Greulich, F.K., Lurye, L.E. and Shrout, P.E. (2007) 'The role of gender constancy in early gender development.' *Child Development 78*, 4, 1121–1136.

5   Gutman, S.A. and Napier-Klemic, J. (1996) 'The experience of head injury on the impairment of gender identity and gender role.' *American Journal of Occupational Therapy 50*, 7, 535–544.

6   Olson, K.R., Durwood, L., DeMeules, M. and McLaughlin, K.A. (2016) 'Mental health of transgender children who are supported in their identities.' *Pediatrics 137*, 3, e20153223.

7   Reed, B., Rhodes, S., Schofield, P. and Wylie, K. (2009) *Gender Variance in the UK: Prevalence, Incidence, Growth and Geographic Distribution*, Gender Identity Research and Education Society. Accessed on 4/12/2018 at http://worldaa1.miniserver.com/~gires/assets/Medpro-Assets/GenderVarianceUK-report.pdf.

8   Equality and Human Rights Commission (2012) *Technical Note: Measuring Gender Identity*. Accessed on 21/03/2019 at https://www.equalityhumanrights.com/en/publication-download/technical-note-measuring-gender-identity.

9   Department for Work and Pensions (2018) *Family Resources Survey: financial year 2016/17*. Accessed on 8/11/2018 at https://assets.publishing.service.gov.uk/government/uploads/system/uploads/attachment_data/file/692771/family-resources-survey-2016-17.pdf.

10 Eurostat (2015) 'Disability statistics – need for assistance.' Accessed on 8/11/2018 at https://ec.europa.eu/eurostat/statistics-explained/index.php/Disability_statistics_-_need_for_assistance#People_with_disabilities_requiring_assistance.

11 Equality Act (2010), Schedule 3, section 27.5. Accessed on 8/11/2018 at www.legislation.gov.uk/ukpga/2010/15/pdfs/ukpga_20100015_en.pdf.

12 Equality Act (2010), Schedule 3, section 28.

13 United Nations (1948) *Universal Declaration of Human Rights*. Accessed on 8/11/2018 at www.un.org/en/universal-declaration-human-rights.

14 Council of Europe (2010) *European Convention on Human Rights*. Accessed on 8/11/2018 at www.echr.coe.int/Documents/Convention_ENG.pdf.

15 Hull, L. (2017) 'Transgender girl, 11, is shot in the shoulder with a BB gun at school after experiencing five months of bullying.' *Daily Mail*, 10 February 2017. Accessed on 8/11/2018 at www.dailymail.co.uk/news/article-4210122/Transgender-girl-11-shot-BB-gun-school.html.

16 Hunt, R. (2017) 'When transphobic people try to pretend they're defending butch lesbians like me, I see the cynical tactic for what it is.' *The Independent*, 16 November 2017.

17 Hands Across the Aisle, a coalition of radical feminists and US Evangelical Christian conservatives who describe trans people as 'extreme' and a 'tyranny'. https://handsacrosstheaislewomen.com/home.

18 Goldberg, M. (2014) 'What is a woman? The dispute between radical feminism and transgenderism.' *The New Yorker*, 4 August 2014. Accessed on 8/11/2018 at www.newyorker.com/magazine/2014/08/04/woman-2.

19 European Society of Endocrinology (2018) 'Transgender brains are more like their desired gender from an early age.' *Science Daily*, 24 May 2018. Accessed on 8 November 2018 at www.sciencedaily.com/releases/2018/05/180524112351.htm.

20 Allen, M. (2008) 'Transgender History: Trans Expression in Ancient Times.' The Bilerico Project, 12 February 2008. Accessed on 8/11/18 at http://bilerico.lgbtqnation.com/2008/02/transgender_history_trans_expression_in.php.

21 Antjoule, N. (2016) *The Hate Crime Report 2016: Homophobia, Biphobia and Transphobia in the UK*. Accessed on 8/11/18 at www.galop.org.uk/wp-content/uploads/2016/10/The-Hate-Crime-Report-2016.pdf.

22 Moser, C. (2010) 'Blanchard's autogynephilia theory: A critique.' *Journal of Homosexuality 57*, 6, 790–809.

23 Littman, L. (2018) 'Rapid-onset gender dysphoria in adolescents and young adults: A study of parental reports.' *PLoS ONE 13*, 8, e0202330. Accessed on 8/11/2018 at https://doi.org/10.1371/journal.pone.0202330.

24 Rudgard, O. (2018) 'Brown University in row with transgender activists over claims gender dysphoria spreading among children.' *The Telegraph*, 28 August 2018. Accessed on 8/11/2018 at www.telegraph.co.uk/news/2018/08/28/ivy-league-college-deletes-link-study-claimed-peer-groups-can.

25 Diamond, M. (2013) 'Transsexuality among twins: Identity concordance, transition, rearing, and orientation.' *International Journal of Transgenderism 14*, 1, 24–38.

26 Barnett, B.S., Nesbit, A.E. and Sorrentino, R.M. (2018) 'The transgender bathroom debate at the intersection of politics, law, ethics, and science.' *Journal of the American Academy of Psychiatry and the Law 46*, 2, 232–241.

27 'How many transgender inmates are there?' BBC Reality Check, 13 August 2018. Accessed on 8/11/2018 at www.bbc.co.uk/news/uk-42221629.

28 Pulk, L. (2014) 'Sexual Assault in the LGBT Community.' National Center for Lesbian Rights. Accessed on 8/11/2018 at www.nclrights.org/sexual-assault-in-the-lgbt-community.

29 Delingpole, J. (2017) 'Justine Greening's idiotic gender policy shows it's time to give up on Toryism.' *The Spectator*, 29 July 2017. Accessed on 8/11/208 at www.spectator.co.uk/2017/07/justine-greenings-idiotic-gender-policy-shows-its-time-to-give-up-on-toryism.

30 Scottish Transgender Alliance (2008) *Transgender Experiences in Scotland*. Accessed on 8/11/2018 at www.scottishtrans.org/wp-content/uploads/2013/03/staexperiencessummary03082.pdf.

31 Department for Work and Pensions/Office for Disability Issues (2014) *Disability Facts and Figures*. Accessed on 8/11/2018 at www.gov.uk/government/publications/disability-facts-and-figures/disability-facts-and-figures.

32 Stonewall (2017) *LGBT in Britain: Trans Report*, p.8. Accessed on 8/11/2018 at www.stonewall.org.uk/sites/default/files/lgbt-in-britain-trans.pdf.

33 Stonewall (2017) LGBT in Britain: Trans Report, p.14. Accessed on 8/11/2018 at www.stonewall.org.uk/sites/default/files/lgbt-in-britain-trans.pdf.

34 Theodostou, L. (2018) 'There's no such thing as a transgender broken arm – trans people deserve fair, non-discriminatory access to services.' *Pink News*, 28 March 2018. Accessed on 08/11/2018 at www.pinknews.co.uk/2018/03/28/theres-no-such-thing-as-a-transgender-broken-arm-trans-people-deserve-fair-non-discriminatory-access-to-services.

35 House of Commons Women and Equalities Committee (2015) Oral Evidence: Transgender Equality Inquiry, HC390, p.19. Accessed on 8/11/2018 at http://data.parliament.uk/writtenevidence/committeeevidence.svc/evidencedocument/women-and-equalities-committee/transgender-equality/oral/21345.html.

36 Age UK (2018) *Transgender Issues and Later Life*. Accessed on 8/11/2018 at www.ageuk.org.uk/globalassets/age-uk/documents/factsheets/fs16_transgender_issues_and_later_life_fcs.pdf.

37 Choudrey, S. (2014) Inclusivity: Supporting BAME Trans People. Accessed on 8/11/2018 at www.gires.org.uk/wp-content/uploads/2016/02/BAME_Inclusivity.pdf.

38 Addlakha, R., Price, J. and Heidari, S. (2017) 'Disability and sexuality: Claiming sexual and reproductive rights.' *Reproductive Health Matters 25*, 50, 4–9.

39 Belcher, H. (2014) *TransDocFail – The Findings*. Accessed on 12/11/2018 at https://challengingjourneys.files.wordpress.com/2014/11/transdocfail-findings.pdf.

40 General Medical Council (2013) *Good Medical Practice*. Accessed on 12/11/2018 at www.gmc-uk.org/-/media/documents/good-medical-practice---english-1215_pdf-51527435.pdf.

41 UK Trans Info (2016) *Current Waiting Times and Patient Population for Gender Identity Clinics in the UK*. Accessed on 12/11/2018 at http://tiac.lgbt/attachments/article/341/patientpopulation-oct15.pdf.

42 Written Evidence submitted by Michael Toze to the Inquiry into Transgender Equality, Michael Toze, July 2015. Accessed on 12/11/2018 at http://data.parliament.uk/writtenevidence/committeeevidence.svc/evidencedocument/women-and-equalities-committee/transgender-equality/written/18822.pdf.

43 The legal approach used to determine the ability of children under 16 to make medical decisions without their parents' involvement. See NSPCC guidance at https://learning.nspcc.org.uk/research-resources/briefings/gillick-competency-and-fraser-guidelines.

44 Carol, 'Gender GP, Helen Webberley is cleared by MPTS.' Transfigurations Blog, 21 March 2018. Accessed on 12/11/2018 at https://blogger.transfigurations.org.uk/2018/03/21/helen-webberley-cleared-by-mpts.

45 Torjesen, I. (2018) 'Trans health needs more and better services: Increasing capacity, expertise, and integration.' *BMJ 362;k3371*. Accessed on 12/11/2018 at www.bmj.com/content/362/bmj.k3371.full.

46 Dhejne, C., Oberg, K., Arver, S. and Landén, M. (2014) 'An analysis of all applications for sex reassignment surgery in Sweden, 1960–2010: Prevalence, incidence, and regrets.' *Archives of Sexual Behavior 43*, 8, 1535–1545.

47 Nissim, M. (2017) 'Trans woman opens up about the death threats that led her to consider abandoning transition.' *Pink News*, 7 August 2017. Accessed on 15/11/2018 at www.pinknews.co.uk/2017/08/07/trans-woman-opens-up-about-the-death-threats-that-led-her-to-consider-abandoning-transition.

48 Chartered Management Institute, 'Disability Discrimination Still Blocking Employee Career Progression.' CMI Insights, 28 November 2016. Accessed on 12/11/2018 at www.managers.org.uk/insights/news/2016/november/disability-discrimination-still-blocking-employee-career-progression.

49 Miller, L.R. and Grollman, E.A. (2015) 'The social costs of gender nonconformity for transgender adults: Implications for discrimination and health.' *Sociological Forum*, doi 10.1111/socf.12193.

50 New York Speech and Voice Lab, 'Masculine voice.' Accessed on 13/11/2018 at www.nyspeechandvoicelab.net/transgender/voice-masculinization.

51 Metro (2016) *National Youth Chances.* Accessed on 4/12/2018 at https://metrocentreonline.org/research/2016/nov/10/national-youth-chances.

52 Hughes, K., Bellis, M.A., Jones, L., Wood, S. *et al.* (2012) 'Prevalence and risk of violence against adults with disabilities: A systematic review and meta-analysis of observational studies.' *The Lancet 379*, 9826, 1621–1629.

53 O'Toole, M. (2015) 'Columnist mocks blind transgender people again, after watchdog complaint.' *Pink News*, 16 October 2015. Accessed on 15/11/2018 at www.pinknews.co.uk/2015/10/16/columnist-mocks-blind-transgender-people-again-after-watchdog-complaint.

54 Bouman, W.P., Claes, L., Brewin, N., Crawford, J.R. *et al.*(2016) 'Transgender and anxiety: A comparative study between transgender people and the general population.' *International Journal of Transgenderism 18*, 1, 16–26.

55 Kranz, G.S., Wadsak, W., Kaufmann, U., Savli, M. *et al.* (2015) 'High-dose testosterone treatment increases serotonin transporter binding in transgender people.' *Biological Psychiatry 78*, 8, 525–533.

56 Colizzi, M., Costa, R., Pace, V. and Todarello, O.J. (2013) 'Hormonal treatment reduces psychobiological distress in gender identity disorder, independently of the attachment style.' *The Journal of Sexual Medicine 10*, 12, 3049–3058.

57 Public Health England (2015) *Disability and Domestic Abuse: Risks, Impacts and Response.* London: Public Health England. Accessed on 15/11/2018 at https://assets.publishing.service.gov.uk/government/uploads/system/uploads/attachment_data/file/480942/Disability_and_domestic_abuse_topic_overview_FINAL.pdf.

58 Reisner, S.L., White Hughto, J.M., Gamarel, K.E., Keuroghlian, A.S., Mizock, L. and Pachankis, J. (2016) 'Discriminatory experiences associated with posttraumatic stress disorder symptoms among transgender adults.' *Journal of Counseling Psychology 63*, 5, 509–519.

59 Stonewall Scotland (2017) *School Report Scotland: The Experiences of Lesbian, Gay, Bi and Trans Young People in Scotland's Schools in 2017*, chapter 7: Wellbeing and Mental Health. Accessed on 15/11/2018 at www.stonewallscotland.org.uk/sites/default/files/school_report_scotland_2017_0.pdf.

60 Whitlock, J., Muehlenkamp, J., Eckenrode, J., Purington, A. *et al.* (2012) 'Nonsuicidal self-injury as a gateway to suicide in young adults.' *Journal of Adolescent Health 52*, 4, 486–492.

61 TENI and Sheffield Hallam University, *Trans Mental Health and Well-being Survey: Self-Harm and Suicide*, September 2012. Accessed on 4/12/2018 at www.teni.ie/attachments/1ceee942-ac62-4dac-8741-5f9e752f3e86.pdf.

62 Meltzer, H., Brugha, T., Dennis, M.S., Hassiotis, A. *et al.* (2012) 'The influence of disability on suicidal behaviour.' *European Journal of Disability Research 6*, 1, 1–12.

63 Bulman, M. and Polianskaya, A. (2017) 'Attempted suicides by disability benefit claimants more than double after introduction of fit-to-work assessment.' *The Independent*, 28 December 2017.

64 Diemer, E.W., Grant, J.D., Munn-Chernoff, M.A., Patterson, D.A. and Duncan, A.E. (2015) 'Gender identity, sexual orientation, and eating-related pathology in a national sample of college students.' *Journal of Adolescent Health 57*, 2, 144–149.

65 Formari, V. and Dancyger, I.F. (2003) 'Psychosexual development and eating disorders.' *Journal of Adolescent Medicine 14*, 1, 61–75.

66 Barbarich-Marsteller, N.C., Foltin, R.W. and Walsh, B.T. (2011) 'Does anorexia nervosa resemble an addiction?' *Current Drug Abuse Reviews 4*, 3, 197–200.

67 Ålgars, M., Alanko, K., Santtila, P. and Sandnabba, N.K. (2012) 'Disordered eating and gender identity disorder: A qualitative study.' *Journal of Eating Disorders 20*, 4, 300–311.

68 Froreich, F.V., Vartanian, L.R., Grisham, J.R. and Touyz, S.W. (2016) 'Dimensions of control and their relation to disordered eating behaviours and obsessive-compulsive symptoms.' *Journal of Eating Disorders 4*, 14. Accessed on 15/11/2018 at https://jeatdisord.biomedcentral.com/articles/10.1186/s40337-016-0104-4.

69 World Health Organization (2019) 'Human papillomavirus (HPV) and cervical cancer.' Accessed on 21/03/2019 at https://www.who.int/news-room/fact-sheets/detail/human-papillomavirus-(hpv)-and-cervical-cancer.

70 'HPV vaccination to be offered to Scottish boys.' *BBC News*, 8 July 2018.

71 'HPV injection to be given to boys, says health secretary.' *BBC News*, 18 July 2018.

72 'Anti-HPV jab will be given to teenage boys…but only if they identify as girls so that "they fit in with their peers".' *Daily Mail*, 3 June 2018.

73 'HPV vaccine to be given to boys in England.' Department of Health and Social Care, 24 July 2018.

74 Stonewall (2018) *Supporting Trans Women in Domestic and Sexual Violence Services: Interviews with Professionals in the Sector.* Accessed on 16/11/2018 at www.stonewall.org.uk/sites/default/files/stonewall_and_nfpsynergy_report.pdf.

75 Roch, R., Morton, J. and Ritchie, G. (2010) *Out of Sight, Out of Mind? Transgender People's Experiences of Domestic Abuse.* Scottish Transgender Alliance/Stop Domestic Abuse. Accessed on 16/11/2018 at www.scottishtrans.org/wp-content/uploads/2013/03/trans_domestic_abuse.pdf.

76 Data Protection Act 1998, accessed on 16/11/2018 at www.legislation.gov.uk/ukpga/1998/29/contents.

77 Gender Recognition Act 2004, accessed on 16/11/2018 at www.legislation.gov.uk/ukpga/2004/7/contents.

78 Information Commissioner's Office – https://ico.org.uk.

79 'Training for staff after transgender person "outed" in surgery waiting room.' *Teeside Live*, 13 August 2018. Accessed on 16/11/2018 at www.gazettelive.co.uk/news/teesside-news/training-staff-after-transgender-person-15024995.

80 Olson, K.R., Durwood, L. and McLaughlin, K.A. (2016) 'Mental health of transgender children who are supported in their identities.' *Pediatrics 137*, 3, e20153223.

81 'Directory of Pink Therapists.' Accessed on 16/11/2018 at www.pinktherapy.com/en-gb/findatherapist.aspx.

82 'A trans woman has to repeatedly come out to her mom with dementia and she always has the same response.' *Buzzfeed*, 28 October 2015. Accessed on 16/11/2018 at www.buzzfeed.com/stephaniemcneal/a-transgender-woman-comes-out-to-her-mom-with-alzheimers-eve?utm_term=.eq0N2xpv9#.awJY4bKB7.

83 GIRES (2017) 'Information and support for families of adult transgender, non-binary and non-gender people.' Accessed on 16/11/2018 at www.gires.org.uk/wp-content/uploads/2016/07/Information-and-support-for-families-of-adult-transgender-non-binary-and-non-gender-people.pdf.

84 Depend, www.depend.org.uk/support.html.

85 Scottish Transgender Alliance (2013) *Transgender People's Experiences of Domestic Abuse.* Accessed on 16/11/2018 at www.scottishtrans.org/wp-content/uploads/2013/03/trans_domestic_abuse.pdf.

86 Office for National Statistics (2015) 'Intimate Personal Violence and Partner Abuse, section 8.' Accessed on 16/11/2018 at https://www.ons.gov.uk/peoplepopulationandcommunity/crimeandjustice/articles/domesticabusefindingsfromthecrimesurveyforenglandandwales/yearendingmarch2017.

87   Albert Kennedy Trust (2015) *LGBT Youth Homelessness: A UK National Scoping of Cause, Prevalence, Response and Outcome.* Accessed on 16/11/2018 at www.akt.org.uk/Handlers/Download.ashx?IDMF=c0f29272-512a-45e8-9f9b-0b76e477baf1.

88   Mermaids, www.mermaidsuk.org.uk.

89   Gendered Intelligence, http://genderedintelligence.co.uk.

90   Guss, C.E., Inwards-Breland, D.J., Ozer, E. and Vance Jr, S.R. (2018) 'Experiences with querying gender identity across seven adolescent medicine sites.' *Journal of Adolescent Health 63,* 4, 506–508.

91   Opening Doors London (2014) *Supporting Older Lesbian, Gay, Bisexual and Transgender People: A Checklist for Social Care Providers.* Accessed on 16/11/2018 at http://openingdoorslondon.org.uk/wp-content/uploads/2014/04/older_lgbt_checklist_for_adult_social_care.pdf.

92   Elizabeth Finn Care and University of Kent (2012) *Benefits Stigma in Britain.* Accessed on 16/11/2018 at wwwturn2us-2938.cdn.hybridcloudspan.com/T2UWebsite/media/Documents/Benefits-Stigma-in-Britain.pdf.

93   Tinson, A., Aldridge, H., Born, T.B. and Hughes, C. (2016) *Disability and Poverty: Why Disability Must Be at the Centre of Poverty Reduction.* New Policy Institute. Accessed on 16/11/2018 at www.npi.org.uk/files/3414/7087/2429/Disability_and_poverty_MAIN_REPORT_FINAL.pdf.

94   Scottish Government (2008) *Challenging Prejudice: Changing Attitudes towards Lesbian, Gay, Bisexual and Transgender People in Scotland.* Accessed on 16/11/2018 at www2.gov.scot/Resource/Doc/212871/0056591.pdf.

Index